PAUL VIRILIO

Paul Virilio
Theorist for an Accelerated Culture

STEVE REDHEAD

EDINBURGH UNIVERSITY PRESS

Edinburgh University Press Ltd
22 George Square, Edinburgh

Typeset in Apollo and Optima Display by
Koinonia, Manchester, and
printed and bound in Great Britain by
The Cromwell Press, Trowbridge, Wilts

A CIP record for this book is available from the British Library

ISBN 0 7486 1927 5 (hardback)
ISBN 0 7486 1928 3 (paperback)

Contents

For Laura and Ellie Redhead

Acknowledgements

In memory of Derek Wynne, a colleague and friend for over twenty-five years. Thanks, also, to Anouk Bélanger, Tara Brabazon, Michael Bracewell, Adam Brown, Alain Ehrenberg, Rick Gruneau, Alan Hunt, Greg Keefe, Melanie Latham, Patrick Mignon, Justin O'Connor, Hillegonda Rietveld, Mireille Silcott, Beverley Skeggs and Gary Wickham for various forms of inspiration, help, support and sustenance during the Virilio 'project'. A 'big shout' going out, too, for the Gallimard bookstore on Boulevard St-Laurent in Montreal, Canada, and the RIBA bookshop at CUBE (Centre for the Understanding of the Built Environment) in Manchester, England. Last but not least, thanks to numerous students and staff at the Culture of Cities project in Montreal and Toronto, Canada, and at the School of Media, Communication and Culture, Murdoch University, Perth, Western Australia.

'Things have become so accelerated that processes are no longer inscribed in a linear temporality, in a linear unfolding of history.'

Jean Baudrillard, *The Vital Illusion*

Introduction

Paul Virilio, so-called high priest of speed, has been dropping 'logic bombs' on us for over thirty years. In these highly idiosyncratic tales of accelerated culture, or what we have called accelerated modernity in the pages of this book, the speed of mass communications as well as the speed of 'things' is what counts. In this scenario we have all become historians of Virilio's instant present, where immediacy, instantaneity and ubiquity rule. But this is not the whole story of either Paul Virilio or accelerated culture.

Paul Virilio is now in his eighth decade. He recently retired from his only academic position as Professor of Architecture at the Special School of Architecture in Paris, France, a post he had held since the late 1960s. On retirement he was nominated Emeritus Professor. Armed with his senior citizen card, he moved from Paris to La Rochelle on the Atlantic coast of France, a considerable upheaval for someone like Virilio who suffers from claustrophobia and rarely travels. He retired, he said at the time, to write a book on 'the accident', a project he had had in mind for over ten years. His haphazard progress towards academic life through the 1950s and 1960s was unusual to say the least and, as we shall see in this book, included a period where he spent his time photographing the wartime German bunkers and a spell where he trained as a stained-glass painter. His ultimate claim to international fame is that he has over many years developed a theory of speed, technology and modernity which, whatever its flaws, is worth taking seriously, even if it is ultimately jettisoned by its once enthusiastic users. This theorising of speed and modernity alone marks him out as a major contemporary thinker.

There are conflicting interpretations of Virilio's theorising in the articles written about his work but essentially Virilio's contention is that the speeding-up of technologies in the twentieth and now twenty-first centuries, especially communications technologies like the internet and e-mail, have tended to abolish time and distance. Speed, for Virilio, has had a largely military gestation. The way in which mass communication has speeded up at the same time has meant, in his view, that old-fashioned industrial war has given way to the information bomb or information war. As military conflict has increasingly become 'war at the speed of light' – as he labelled the first Gulf War in the early 1990s – the tyranny of distance in civilian as well as military life has almost disappeared. However, this does not mean that there is no deceleration or slowness. Inertia, or what Virilio termed 'polar inertia', has set in for even the supersonic air traveller or high-speed train devotee. As we have noted, Paul Virilio eventually left his post in academia to write a long-planned book on what he has called the accident, a concept which has become more prevalent in his thinking over the last decade. It is often reflected upon in his discussion of different aspects of the body of his ideas in interview (1998a, 1999a, 2000a, 2000b, 2001a, 2002). It is also an idea which encapsulates some of his most specific pronouncements about speed, technology and modernity. The accident, however, is a very specific term in Virilio's work and suffers in the translation from the French. There is a philosophical dimension to the concept as we shall discover in later chapters in this book. Moreover, the everyday use of the word in English is not really what Virilio has in mind. Suffice to say here that technologies contain within them the capacity to self-destruct. Planes crash, for example. Skyscrapers collapse. And so on.

Virilio predicted the onset of a situation in global culture where there would be an 'accident of accidents': the 'global accident' or the 'total accident', even the 'Great Accident'; that is, an accident occurring everywhere at the same time. An example of Virilio's notion of the accident is the attack on the World Trade Center on 11 September 2001, where he perceived 'a fatal confusion between the attack and the accident' where the 'attack and the accident become indistinguishable'. Speaking to Sylvère Lotringer in Paris in May 2002, some nine months after the event, Virilio noted that 'the door is open' with what he called 'the great attack'. For him, 'September 11 opened Pandora's Box'. In 'this new situation', according to Virilio, 'New York is what Sarajevo was' when 'Sarajevo triggered the First World War'. Virilio proclaimed that New York was 'an act of total war', 'the attack in the first war of globalisation'. This example of the accident as a new form of warfare is appropriate for a snapshot of the potential application of Virilio's ideas to the analysis of a media event. However, care must be taken. We shall pursue this theme in more depth later in this book but '9/11' fits the framework of Virilio's idea of the accident of accidents, although not necessarily in the way it might appear at first sight. For Virilio the new communication technologies such as satellite, digital and other broadcasting mechanisms have changed the world in such a way that what was once a local accident or an event situated in time and space is actually global, occurring everywhere at the same time. Thus, the spectacle of two of the world's tallest buildings burning, and subsequently collapsing, killing almost 3,000 people, was not simply a local, catastrophic event but a global 'accident' shown 'live' to billions of people around the world at the same moment. Almost everyone, everywhere, all over the earth was watching live on either television or computer screens. Virilio calls the virtual territory created by this broadcasting of a live event the 'city of the instant'.

So speed kills. But in Virilio's book speed also enables us to see, and foresee. It changes our 'logistics of perception', our way of seeing, our vision thing. Let us take a more prosaic example, culled from popular culture, although Virilio, it should be noted, rarely takes notice of 'low' culture at all. Consider the case of the speeding-up of sport in modernity. The spectator at a Premiership professional soccer match in England at the beginning of the twenty-first century is witnessing a spectacle which is highly accelerated in all sorts of ways compared even to a match played at the beginning of the Premiership itself only a decade earlier. Ten years ago such matches in England were played at a very high pace in the first half and then, after everyone had had a breather at half time, proceeded to speed up until around three-quarters of the game had been played. This in itself was in great contrast to the way Football League First Division games had been played for over 100 years. In 'modern' soccer culture, essentially since the 1960s, technological changes in the sort of footwear worn, the ball used, the shorts and shirts chosen, grass (or other surface) played on, and floodlighting employed, not to mention training regimes for players, have had the overall effect of speeding up the process of the game to the extent that there is now literally no stopping for ninety minutes. A spectator at a Premiership match today consequently watches, from an inert, sedentary position in a seat (mostly!), an accelerated, and accelerating, spectacle flash by in a blur like the lightweight ball itself. This sporting spectacle is beamed around the globe 'live' to watching millions, be they in Singapore airport or a suburban house in Montreal, by virtue of the global communications revolution also ushered in since the increasing ubiquity of television in the 1960s. Moreover, the way the spectator watching 'live' at the stadium actually sees the speeding spectacle is conditioned by decades of watching such matches 'live' on television, sofa-surfing in the sedentary comfort of his or her armchair. At many grounds, too, the spectator can watch 'live' (with slight delay) replays of the action on giant screens at one end of the ground just in case 'nodding-off', or what Virilio refers to as 'picnolepsy', has occurred. The example we have cited of Premiership soccer in England would thus far fit the notion of an accelerated culture found in very different language and different instances in the work of Paul Virilio. But this is a cautionary tale too, because there is in fact no inexorability about the process we have described. For instance, top league professional soccer in other countries – say Argentina, Japan, Italy or Spain – is not necessarily as fast as the Premiership in England. Soccer style, culture, tradition and tactics in these other countries determine a slower pace of the spectacle even though the same technological changes we have mentioned persist. Moreover, the 'live' televising of English Premiership soccer matches around the globe is often subject to delay, not only the slight 'digital delay', which means a fractional time of delay in the arrival of a signal or message, but the organisational delay of broadcasters in other countries showing 'live' matches delayed by a few minutes, hours or even days to fit in with domestic television schedules ('as live', as they are referred to in the industry). The point of this cautionary tale is partly to underline the familiarity of much of what Virilio has been telling us about speed, technology and modernity for more than the last thirty years. But it is also to serve as a warning that all might not be as it seems in this supposed accelerated culture of the instant present.

This book serves as the first single-authored introduction to Paul Virilio. It is also a critical review of his work in the context of the literature available to date in English but with reference to the full works of Virilio in French. It is the first book to consider the whole of Virilio's oeuvre in the original French and its various translations into English. The Bibliography at the end of the book includes selected bibliographical work of, and on, Virilio. Much of the extraneous material in the Bibliography, such as interviews and critical commentary, is used throughout the book in order to build a picture of Virilio's life and work. Virilio is the author of numerous books and hundreds of articles and reviews, not to mention various collaborations and forewords or introductions to other authors' works, so a comprehensive bibliography would be outside the scope of this book. But the Bibliography in this book can be used as a guide, or a directory, to the most important works by Virilio. It also covers the most revealing interviews with Virilio and the sharpest critical commentaries. As can be seen from the Bibliography, only three of Virilio's many single-authored major texts remain fully untranslated from French into English.

Aimed at readers across a number of academic disciplines and areas of interest throughout the world, the book seeks to situate Paul Virilio's writing and thinking in the pantheon of critical thought. It aims to be an accessible and introductory book but also an intellectually rigorous text in its approach to the whole of Virilio's life and thought. Even though Virilio promises in his writings to create an overarching system of thought, in fact much of his contribution to knowledge is fragmented. Even notions such as 'dromology' (the study of speed) and 'dromocracy' (a society of speed), which might have fulfilled such a grand plan, framework or model for 'Virilian' thought to be poured into, remain tentative. Therefore this book creates and develops new concepts such as accelerated modernity, dangerous modernity and critical modernity which are generated out of the work of Virilio as well as others working in related fields. These concepts help to place Virilio in contradistinction to theorists and figures to whom he has been unhelpfully compared, such as Michel Foucault, Jean Baudrillard and Noam Chomsky. They also highlight contradictions and non-sequiturs in Virilio's body of work as well as the insights he has made.

Chapter 1 considers the reasons in general why we might need to remember Paul Virilio as a major contemporary thinker in the future. In pinpointing these reasons it tells the outline story of Virilio's life, work and career. Born in France in the early 1930s and growing up in the context of the German military forces' dominance of the country during the Second World War, Virilio became a committed Christian at the age of eighteen. The chapter concentrates on the 1950s and 1960s, a period which has often been neglected in previous assessments or discussions of Virilio. In the 1950s Virilio scoured the northern French coastal beaches for the German bunkers remaining from the Second World War. He photographed them in their hundreds and wrote about their architectural and technological significance in an embryonic theory he called 'bunker archaeology' and later 'cryptic architecture'. Unlike many of the other French theorists of his generation, he began his studies in a personalised, informal way, but the work was to influence his thinking in the academy for the rest of his life. However, in Virilio's unusual trajectory his academic period did not start until the end of the 1960s when he was in his late thirties. In the 1960s, as well as studying at the university of the Sorbonne in Paris, and further becoming a painter of stained glass, he joined forces with an older professional architect, Claude Parent. Although he never qualified as an architect, Virilio and Parent were a potent practical and theoretical force and their ideas shook up established French, and other cultures', thinking on architecture for a time. Then May 1968 occurred and nothing was quite the same again for Virilio. Much of this period – the 1950s and 1960s – of Virilio's personal and political biography has remained as forgotten as the German bunkers which prompted the journey in the first place. Chapter 1 contextualises all of this personal history and looks ahead to the rich publishing future of Virilio's next three decades.

Chapter 2 considers Virilio's place as the 'high priest of speed'. The chapter shows that this can be slowness or fastness, and moreover that instantaneity and ubiquity are key processes in the disappearance of time and space which Virilio predicts. Looking at the development in chronological order of his French and English publications and interviews on speed, the chapter sets Virilio's ideas in a more theorised and fluid picture of what this book calls accelerated culture, or accelerated modernity. Virilio did not register an 'epistemological break' in his work and much of the work from the 1950s and 1960s discussed in Chapter 1 is shown to be coterminous with the continuing interest in the body and speed which he pursued for the next three decades. There is considerable development of the ideas as Virilio's academic and intellectual career goes forward. The chapter pursues both critical and appreciative commentaries on Virilio, as well as various interviews with him over the years, in order to assess the overall value of what Virilio has self-labelled as dromology and the speeding-up of processes such as military technology.

Chapter 3 introduces the notion of dangerous modernity to look at the consequences of the accelerated modernity introduced and considered in Chapter 2. Theorists like Francis Fukuyama and Noam Chomsky are distinguished from Paul Virilio in assessing what is happening at the end of what Virilio refers to as 'a world' (rather than *the* world): in other words the twentieth century of, in his pertinent phrase, 'hyperviolence'. Paul Virilio has written about many media events in his long career as a public intellectual but, as we have noted, the 11 September 2001 attacks on the World Trade Center twin towers in New York, and the Pentagon in Washington, provide a showcase for his thinking better than any other. They highlight his favourite topics of architecture and speed. In fact, he did write at the time about the unsuccessful attempt in 1993 to blow up the World Trade Center. He was even employed as a consultant following that first attack. Virilio has had the chance to speak and write about the '9/11' events briefly and obliquely (2001b, 2002, Virilio 2002a, Virilio 2003b), even contributing to a technical engineering analysis on French radio of the collapse of the twin towers, but this chapter devotes itself to looking at how some of Virilio's ideas fit into the understanding of such an event using what we know about the tragedy itself as a case study. Again, critical and appreciative commentaries and interviews with him on past events are used to interweave Virilio's sporadic thinking on such matters with the actual unfolding of '9/11'. Virilio's notion of the accident is the theme for the chapter, and the reader unfamiliar with any of Virilio's work can glimpse how he might be 'used' in analysis of media events. Whether we think he should be so 'applied' is another matter. In any case, in this chapter Paul Virilio is revealed to be most prominently of all a media theorist of sorts and an interpreter of what he has come to call the global or total accident.

Chapter 4 considers Virilio the art, film, dance, photography, theatre and television theorist in the context of the notion of critical modernity. Critical modernity is actually a concept which has been written about by Virilio's erstwhile architectural partner, Claude Parent, but it is adapted and reworked in this chapter to assess the usefulness of Virilio's aesthetic, cultural and political theories. Frequently Virilio has been seen as falling within the camp of post-modernism or postmodernists. This chapter reviews such critical commentary and compares Virilio with another French theorist who has been labelled in a similar vein across a variety of disciplines – namely Jean Baudrillard. Virilio's political, religious and philoso-phical positions are explicated and taken into account, while what he has written and said about modernity and postmodernity, modernism and postmodernism are hauled over the coals. Critical and appreciative commentaries and interviews with Virilio are once again used to place Virilio in a continuum of critical thinking on modernity. This book argues for Virilio to be seen as a modernist.

Chapter 5 asks whether we should in fact forget Paul Virilio. Something of an overall assessment of his strengths and weaknesses as a theorist is made in this chapter. Virilio's 'traces' are seen to be everywhere in disciplines across the academy, and even his connection to popular culture, a subject on which he has had little to say over the years, is plotted. Acceleration rather than globalisa-tion is seen to be Virilio's personal prediction for the twenty-first century in one of the most heated conflicts amongst major contem-porary commentators today. A number of other academic and political debates are cited as the reader is reminded of the gaps in Virilio's thinking when compared with many younger contemp-orary social and cultural theorists across the globe. The question whether we must forget Paul Virilio as well as remember him is answered after a fashion, and the chapter recalls the early Virilio in the work of the late Virilio, for better or worse.

For the first time then, in the light of all the considerable output of Paul Virilio, this book offers a unique, rounded historical por-trayal of Virilio as an intellectual figure. It is less important that we know he has suffered from asthma, has a daughter, is grey and balding, rarely watches television or has never qualified as an architect, so a Virilio life story will have to wait for another day. For the time being, reading the myriad texts of Virilio (including his many 'live' conversations) helps to situate him in a continuum of public intellectuals from France as well as elsewhere. Paul

Virilio, whatever our ultimate judgement of his worth, has undoubtedly earned his place in a list of contemporary social and cultural theorists and commentators. Compared to his compatriot Jean Baudrillard, Paul Virilio is still perhaps not as prominent in such lists as he might be. That is unlikely to remain the case for long.

CHAPTER ONE

Remember Virilio

Paul Virilio was born in Paris, France in 1932. Paris remained his home for most of his adult life although he moved to the Atlantic coast at La Rochelle on retirement. His father was an Italian communist from Genoa who was an illegal alien in the country and his mother was a Catholic from Brittany. The family lived in the North Atlantic region during the Second World War and in many ways Virilio has dedicated his life and work to an analysis of the unfolding of the consequences of the violence and speed of that terrible conflict. For thirty years from 1969 he was a Professor of Architecture in Paris in the wake of the events which have come to be known as 'May '68', where students and workers in many countries, especially France, rose up and for a brief moment threatened the social order of Western capitalism. It has taken a good many years but today Virilio is at last regarded as a significant contemporary thinker, although what he has actually said and the order in which he said it remains a mystery to many who use his name. There are all kinds of different and surprising influences on his life and thought which help to explain his unique place as a critical thinker: for instance, in this chapter we will consider religion, war, contemporary architecture and French postwar politics.

Christianity

At the age of eighteen Paul Virilio became a Christian and a Catholic 'militant', and he has long proclaimed his religious faith openly. 'I am a Christian' is a frequent unambiguous statement in interviews, without any apparent concern for the approbation of fashionable interviewers, sceptical critics or even erstwhile followers. In an age when political leaders such as George Bush, Bill Clinton, George W. Bush and Tony Blair actively promote themselves as Christian believers whilst unleashing massive military operations against Afghanistan, Iraq and the former Yugoslavia, which Virilio himself has criticically analysed and frequently condemned in the strongest terms, labels such as 'Christian' and 'religious' have become major battlegrounds in themselves. Paul Virilio has had no time at all for the religion-driven 'new world order' initiated by the Christian George Bush, former CIA chief, nor the version of it carried on by the self-proclaimed Christians Tony Blair and Bill Clinton. Virilio has sharply analysed what he called the 'secular holy war' with its 'fundamentalist' 'duty to intervene' conducted by NATO in the Balkans in the 1990s. He has also unmasked, in his words, 'the tragi-comic infantilisation' of the century's end which involved Bill Clinton and 'Monicagate', a media event which had the consequence of denuding the US president of power and authority to such an extent that Virilio wondered aloud whether he had 'not already been discreetly removed from office' for the last couple of years of his second term as the military personnel mocked him. Virilio was acutely aware that this infantilisation involved a scenario where 'like the child in the playpen' the war leader 'wants to try out everything, show off everything, for fear of otherwise seeming weak and isloated'. End-of-the-century American techno-logy, in the form of 'smart' cruise missiles, F 117s and B52 bombers, has been used in Virilio's eyes as if 'the world were a toy or a war game'. The twenty-first century has started in exactly the same manner, with the 'war on terror' in Afghanistan even extending the 'war game' with the development, and use, of new military technologies to blow up mountains and caves where Islamic funda-mentalist fighters were thought to be hiding. Virilio could not have been more critical of this kind of Christianity.

As Virilio has said, 'the ironic outcome of techno-scientific development' like the cruise and other missiles employed against Bin Laden, Saddam, Milosevic and others is a 'renewed need for the idea of God'. Paul Virilio's Christian beliefs – emphasising 'Incarna-tion not Resurrection' – echo the tradition of theologians Jacques Ellul and Pierre Teilhard de Chardin, proponents of a Christian existentialism. For Canadian theorist Arthur Kroker, this tradition of Christian dissent, especially where it operates – as Kroker sees it – against the totalitarianism of technology, can be seen as a positive aspect to Virilio's religious conviction. Others are less generous and see it as Virilio's Achilles' heel, especially in his theoretical formu-lations, even if they would grant him some political exemptions for opposition to the 'new world order'. Still others would attack Virilio for his Catholicism and the anti-statism which goes along with it. The state and power are, as we shall see in this book, problematic concepts in Virilio's work.

Although we shall argue in this book that Virilio does not believe in anything after modernity – postmodernity, for instance – death, in its many forms, holds almost an obsessive interest for him. His religious beliefs underlie this interest but death is also a pervasive concept in Virilio's work. 'Picnolept', for example, in Virilio's theoretical vocabulary stands for a state of temporary 'death' or sub-epileptic unconsciousness, a kind of checking-out for a moment before consciousness reigns again. Human life in the modern condition is interrupted by these tiny deaths, before the ultimate death, in Virilio's vision. But because of Virilio's religious faith, even this death is not real for human beings. Neither – despite news to the contrary for much of the twentieth century – is God 'dead'. For Virilio, 'God has come back into history through the door of terror'; contrary to Nietzsche, he has maintained that 'God isn't dead':

> Personally I'm at odds with this question of death. Why? Because on the one hand I'm a Christian, thus I don't believe in death, but in the soul's immortality; on the other hand, I don't want to use this faith with respect to those who don't share it. And finally because I don't believe that faith should be an instrument: that would be the worst kind of belief, from which you get the Holy War, religious terrorism, etc. So my return to death is a reflection of disappearance, on the final outcome, on the end, on the fact that what IS will cease to exist, on interruption. Whence, PICNOLEPSY, little death, etc ... My way of approaching death is both physical and metaphysical. I'm faced here with a problem of writing because I can't hide the fact that I'm a Christian (I don't see why I should hide it, for me it's essential) but on the other hand I don't want to use this 'advantage' to challenge things that are common to believers and non-believers alike. (Virilio 1997a: 128–9)

Virilio, curiously, still sees himself as a 'materialist of the body' amidst his religious conviction. For him, 'Man is God, and God is Man, the world is nothing but the world of Man – or Woman. So to separate mind from body doesn't make any sense.' In most senses, however, Virilio is an idealist rather than a materialist in the philosophical sense. He has never been a Marxist, or any kind of historical materialist, and his philosophical training at the university of the Sorbonne in Paris was phenomenological and centred on the psychology of perception. 'Idealism', in the sense of wanting a better, reformed world, has also driven Virilio on since his youth and has persisted in his later years.

Personally Virilio has always been interested in deeds of social reform. He has, for instance, sat on the French commission concerned with housing the poor, chaired by Louis Besson, for over a decade. Individually, too, Virilio has for a long time been inspired by the Abbé Pierre and the movement of worker-priests. The Abbé Pierre is a popular French priest who campaigned for the poor and who met in the 1950s another of Virilio's influences, the scientist Albert Einstein. The Abbé Pierre, however, eventually became controversial in France because of his backing of a revisionist view of the Nazi Holocaust against the Jews in the Second World War. The worker-priests' movement consisted of an attempt by the Catholic church to, in a sense, 'reclaim the working class' after the Second World War by sending priests to work in the factories. The Christian religion, then, has ever since that period of his youth been dominant in Paul Virilio's life in terms of his strong personal faith and his active concern for the homeless and the poor. His work for the homeless, the *sans-logis*, began as long ago as the winter of 1954. He has ever since been on a *'voyage d'hiver'* and eventually was involved in creating a social service for the homeless. However, as we have indicated, the philosophical aspects of religion, and the conception of the human being in religion, are more complex as far as Virilio is concerned.

In actuality Virilio has a concept of death as accident, or as interruption of knowledge, which spreads throughout his work, not just in his own religious faith. For example, his notion of the consciousness of the human subject under God, and moreover of death itself, is not necessarily a conventional one. The concept of the 'picnolept' has marked out his thinking. Although he has eschewed the pyschoanalytical thinking of his fellow countryman Jacques Lacan and all other practitioners of what he regards as a kind of black art, he does conceive of human subjectivity in theoretical terms, however crude this may seem when compared to the sophisticated and dense thought systems of many other French theorists. Essentially, his main idea of the modern condition for the human 'subject' has been one of 'picnolepsy', which is best understood in layperson's language as a kind of micro-sleep or a momentary lapse of consciousness or temporary 'disappearance'. In fact, although mentioned in his short discourse on religion and death, 'picnolepsy' is quite generally applied, in a more secular way, in his writing and thinking on speed and modernity, on war and technology, and on what he has conceived of as the aesthetics of disappearance. For example, he has recalled that:

> In *The Aesthetics of Disappearance* … the main idea is the social and political role of stopping. The break taken for sleep has been worked on a lot for psychoanalysis, but I have absolutely no confidence in psychoanalysis. In fact, all interruptions interest me, from the smallest to the largest, which is death. Death is an interruption of knowledge. All interruptions are. And it's because there is an interruption of knowledge that a time proper to it is constituted. The rhythm of the alternation of consciousness and unconsciousness is 'picnolepsy', the picnoleptic interruption (from the Greek picnos, 'frequent'), which helps us exist in a duration which is our own, of which we are conscious. All interruptions structure this consciousness and idealise it … Epilepsy is little death and picnolepsy, tiny death. What is living, present, conscious here, is only so because there's an infinity of little deaths, little accidents, little breaks, little cuts in the sound track, as William Burroughs would say, in the sound track and the visual track of what's lived. And I think that's very interesting for the analysis of the social, the city, politics. (Virilio 1997a: 39–40)

It is ironic perhaps that a theorist known and celebrated for his interest in accelerated culture and speed of and in modernity should so frequently remind us of the importance of stopping, interruption and partial death. The link between these poles – of inertia and absolute speed – does not disappear from Paul Virilio's theoretical landscape and is ever present in his thinking.

War baby

For Virilio, looking back on his life, 'war' not religion was his most lasting influence. War – the Second World War – was his 'father' and 'mother', as he has said in interview. War, where 'death literally fell from the skies', baptising 'by fire', was his 'trauma' and 'birth'. He was 'formed by war', experiencing 'the war in Nantes, a city with armament factories and a submarine port, which was destroyed by air raids'. He even began to write, as a ten-year-old boy, about the 'destruction' of the city, keeping a notebook of the times, of 'war and the city'. In his phrase, 'war was my university', echoing the attitudes of some writers towards the Spanish Civil War. In fact, Virilio 'fought in the Algerian War, as a draftee' but in a number of ways it was the Second World War, especially in France and even more specifically in the North Atlantic region, which was to have a lifelong and demonstrably profound effect on 'Paul Virilio' the cultural theorist as well as the man. Seven years old at the beginning of the conflict, Virilio has frequently described himself in English and even when speaking in French as a 'Blitzkrieg baby' or a 'war baby'. He exclaimed, in conversation with fellow countryman Philippe Petit, 'Si je travaille sur les questions militaires, comme André Glucksmann ou Alain Joxe, c'est parce que je suis un WAR BABY' (original version, Virilio 1999: 94). To work on 'military problems' because he was a 'war baby', like such 'intellectuals of defense' as the political author and academic Alain Joxe (with whom he later worked from the late 1970s in Joxe's 'Sociology of Defense' group) and the 'New Philosopher' André Glucksmann, obviously made eminent sense to Virilio. He has also recalled that the pyschological effect was that he 'was terrorised by war'. 'As a child I suffered the war: the destruction of the city of Nantes when I was ten was a traumatic event for me', he told long-time interviewer Sylvère Lotringer in a series of early 1980s interviews for Semiotext(e), the New York publishing venture which brought Virilio to an English-speaking audience for the first time. He talked in these fascinating and wide-ranging Lotringer interviews about what he called 'pure war', or the way in which war continued after 'total war' had ended. Legally, too, Virilio has argued that the Second World War has 'not finished'. It has not 'been put out'. In Virilio's language, 'there's no state of peace'. The Second World War is not over for Virilio because 'it continued in Total Peace, that is in war pursued by other means'.

So gripped was Virilio by this legacy of the Second World War that for ten years from the 1950s he began studying military architecture and 'looked for elements of the European Fortress'.

Paul Virilio, still in these pioneering early studies apparently an obsessive young man in search of the meaning of the warfare which had so traumatised the population of his region, devoted himself in the 1950s and early 1960s to compulsively researching the brutalist architecture of the Second World War German bunkers. This gave rise to what was to become a distinct Virilian trope: a veritable 'bunker archaeology', which was to extend beyond the book of the same title and dominate his thinking at least until the mid 1970s. In fact, *Bunker Archéologie*, or *Bunker Archaeology* in English translation, was first published as an illustrated book in French in 1975, but a very short, personal, pioneering piece, first written in 1958, saw the light of day in 1966. Virilio began his research into the bunkers in 1958 – the date of a supposed revelation he had on a beach in Normandy – and he saw 'the blueprint of the blockhouse' as 'strangely reminiscent of Aztec temples'. The project of the 'architecture of war' had begun for Virilio, and it led in later life to his works being 'read seriously by the French military'. He started in this 1950s project to look at war as a military 'space'. Virilio has admitted that he had no social sciences background, no training in the 'sociology of war' or the 'history of technology'. His 'war' experience was mainly 'living' it through the Second World War and its aftermath (and a brief time as a draftee later on in the Algerian War). The German bunkers, and the systematic photographs he took of them, were the start of a career for Virilio, concentrating on military space. As he has intimated, it was more than the object of study that interested him:

> It's not by chance that I studied the Atlantic Wall. I didn't study the blockhouses, I studied their position. I studied the wall, the circle of blockhouses, everything that happens between the continental space and the maritime space. Later I went to see the Siegfried Line and the Maginot Line, but after the Atlantic Wall: I never would have wanted to go beforehand. It's because I was interested in the coastal region. For me the coastal region is an amazing thing, a marvellous interruption, an interface as they say. I've always thought in terms of breaks, in terms of either/or, in terms of the dividing line of waters – those places where things are exchanged, transformed. (Virilio 1997a: 115)

Thus for Virilio the archaeology of the bunker implied more than an aesthetic interest in military relics. It was already an architectural and design interest, which was to be transformed into what he called a theory of the 'oblique', or the inclined plane, during the 1960s. The 'end of verticality' and the 'end of horizontality', which Virilio proclaimed in the 1960s as part of his architectural theory revolution, were first touched on in these early explorations of 'bunker archaeology' and its various associated practices. The more general forays into what he came to call the 'function of the oblique' became subsequently much more emphatic in the urban Parisian architectural milieu of the 1960s but the rural seaside photographs he took of the German bunkers contained many of the seeds of this later work. Such military bunker themes have 'obliquely' infused Virilio's later theoretical writings in other areas. Put simply, Virilio used the military architecture of the bunkers and developed, dialectically, a way of ending the right angle (the horizontal and vertical meeting point) and replacing it, architecturally, with an incline, or the oblique. Paul Virilio has explained that:

> Since 1958 I had been studying not only the blockhouses of the Atlantic Wall and the Siegfried and Maginot lines, but also the military spaces of what was known as 'Fortress Europe', with its rocket-launching sites, air-defence systems, autobahns and radar stations. This was an archaeological study, and a personal one, motivated by the desire to uncover the geostrategic and geopolitical foundations of the total war I had lived through as a young boy in Nantes, not far from the submarine base of Saint-Nazaire. For me, the architecture of war made palpable the power of technology – and the now infinite power of destruction. (Virilio and Parent 1996: 11)

Once again, the personal was the inspiration for the theoretical. Virilio had escaped with his family from the Gestapo in Nantes in 1941, partly owing to what he later called in his theoretical writing the 'cryptic architecture' of his family home. The architectural archaeology he began in 1958, stimulated by these childhood memories of German invasion and the military architecture which went with it, ended formally in 1965. By then he had not only completed the initial bunker archaeology project in France but from 1960 onwards had made several field trips to Germany to consult archives and to study the anti-aircraft shelters of the major German

cities and the Maginot and Siegfried lines. Such interests have
sustained his work on war and technology throughout his life. For
instance, books on the Gulf War and the NATO bombing of Serbia
over Kosovo in the 1990s drew on ideas first formulated in his
'bunker archaeology' period. Books and an exhibition were given
over to the extensive studies he made up and down the Atlantic
Wall which had produced his idiosyncratic photographs of thousands of German bunkers. This work may have been borne out of
almost a hobby but the deep legacy of the 'early' work, visual and
written, never really leaves Virilio. A full English translation of this
1950s bunker project was not available to scholars until 1994, by
which time all kinds of wild interpretations of Virilio and his
cultural significance had been ventured. This English translation,
Bunker Archaeology (Virilio 1994b), was in any case taken from the
second, revised, expanded version of *Bunker Archéologie*, published in 1991 in France rather than the 1975 original. In fact, as we
can see with hindsight, the bunker archaeology period was long-
lasting.

Today we are in a position to see more clearly the impact of the
'total war' of the Second World War on Virilio's thinking in whatever sphere he was to subsequently interrogate in his theoretical
work or his teaching, be it architecture, photography, cinema or
contemporary art. As Virilio was to say much later in his 'war
career', the 'essence of war' and the 'essence of cinema' are related,
and the only question is how much.

Architecture cryptique

As well as photographing thousands of German bunkers, by the
early 1960s Virilio had trained as a painter and an artist in stained
glass. He went to study at the Ecole des Métiers d'Art in Paris, the
city where he was born and which remained his home until the end
of the twentieth century. He was at this time working as a painter,
mainly in order to earn a living, and, among other work, produced
designs for Braque, at Varengeville, and Matisse, at Saint-Paul-de-
Vence. Virilio has said that he has continued to approach everything as a visual artist and has gone so far as to admit that he always
writes 'with images – I cannot write a book if I don't have images'.

It was this aesthetic perspective which was to pervade all that followed in Paul Virilio's subsequent academic career despite efforts by many commentators and critics to pigeonhole his position in specific social or human sciences. The erasure of his original aesthetic background in many of the surveys of Virilio's work to date over the years is nevertheless understandable. He did indeed take the opportunity while in Paris in the early 1960s to study philosophy at the university of the Sorbonne, where he became passionate about architecture and the psychology of form, taking courses by the likes of the sociologist Raymond Aron, the existentialist philosophers Vladimir Jankelevitch and Jean Wahl, and, most significantly, the influential French phenomenologist Maurice Merleau-Ponty. Virilio has said that he was a 'follower of *Gestalttheorie*' and that he audited Merleau-Ponty's late lectures before he died in 1961. Merleau-Ponty's perspective in particular does not really fade from Virilio's work. The Husserlian phenomenology, which Merleau-Ponty promoted, based its philosophy in bodily behaviour and perception. It reappears often in Virilio's writing and is the source of criticism from those who see in his work a tendency to put forward an idealist, as opposed to a materialist Marxist position, which needs 'standing on its head'. Virilio has himself openly admitted that he has been a 'man of the percept as well as the concept'.

In this brief biographical scenario Virilio might seem to fit the trajectory of so many other French 'philosophers' of the twentieth and twenty-first centuries, but actually he differs considerably. The intellectual figures with whom he is regularly bracketed frequently had highly academic careers that went uninterrupted over decades from their youthful student days. While these intellectuals were moving and shaking in their universities, Virilio, as he has plaintively noted, simply 'made paintings'. Virilio's 'bunker man' period was followed by a painting and stained-glass training and practice that were distinctly unusual. Although he was eventually a full-time academic for a long period – for all of thirty years in fact – Virilio's trajectory was very different to that of the French theorists with whom he has often been compared and contrasted, such as Louis Althusser, Jean Baudrillard or Michel Foucault. In Virilio's case, too, apart from the brief philosophical interlude at the Sorbonne, his previous and subsequent work was not really produced in any discourse resembling 'philosophy'.

For one thing, as distinct from other French theorists who have become key contemporary thinkers, Paul Virilio became immersed in the then less-than-fashionable world of 1960s French architecture. Eventually developing it formally as his academic profession as a Professor of Architecture, Paul Virilio was awarded the Laureate of the Grand Prix National de la Critique Architecturale in France in 1987. As the Director of the Ecole Spéciale d'Architecture in Paris, a post which essentially stemmed from 1972 when he was made co-director, he was Professor of Architecture for three decades and eventually President of the Ecole for many years. He retired from the Special School of Architecture only at the close of the 1990s when he was in his late sixties. Curiously, however, he never formally qualified as an architect at any time. His later role at the Special School of Architecture was as an architecture theorist and teacher, a trainer of architects, as he has noted, for the real world.

Virilio's architectural adventures began as early as the beginning of the 1960s. In 1963 he formed the 'Architecture Principe' group with Claude Parent, an architect, Michael Carrade, a painter, and Morice Lipsi, a sculptor. The aim was to investigate and promote a new kind of architectural and urban order. The group lasted until 1968–9 when Claude Parent and Paul Virilio fell out over Virilio's participation in the momentous and, as far as he was concerned, long-lasting events of 'May '68'. As for the journal/magazine entitled *Architecture Principe*, only Claude Parent and Paul Virilio put their signatures to the short articles in the publication which constituted its permanent manifesto. From fragile beginnings, nine numbered issues of *Architecture Principe* were published between February and December 1966, as well as a final number ten, an anniversary issue in September 1996, thirty years later. Each of the original 'Architecture Principe' (literally Architecture (in) Principle, but essentially urging architecture to begin again) manifestos had a specific title. These were: 'The Oblique Function', 'The Third Urban Order', 'Potentialism', 'The Nevers Worksite', 'Habitable Circulation', 'The Mediate City', 'Bunker Archaeology', 'Power and Imagination', and 'Blueprint for Charleville'. These themes made up the first nine issues, all published in the mid 1960s. 'Disorientation or

Dislocation' was the title of the tenth and last issue in 1996. By today's publishing standards the magazine's issues were short on word length but high on rhetoric and conceptual innovation. For instance, issue seven of *Architecture Principe*, 'Bunker Archaeology', was published in September/October 1966. It comprised the short essay by Paul Virilio, entitled 'Bunker Archaeology', which actually dated from 1958. This was followed by another short essay from Virilio written in September 1965, entitled 'Cryptic Architecture', which contained enigmatic statements such as (in English translation from the original French of the manifesto) 'cities are episodic and cerebral, they are a permanent and genetic crypt', 'cryptic architecture is thus an infra-architecture' and 'cryptic energy, itself indissociable from the survival of all living species'. 'Architecture Cryptique' was the label Paul Virilio used in the early to mid 1960s for the theoretical ideas spawned by his 'bunker archaeology'. Claude Parent's contribution to issue seven was only slightly more than three short paragraphs. He proclaimed, several years before Virilio actually gained an academic post, that 'Paul Virilio is a reader of reality. He holds the university chair of the real; he is not in the analytical domain, but is a creator. In the present he is hunting for future portents. He sifts, chooses, gathers.' Parent went on in this brief, bizarre, but strangely accurate eulogy to describe Virilio as a 'man of faith' and 'in a state of permanent disequilibrium' who 'in order to triumph over original sin' has 'us discover today the masterpieces of an ancient world of terror'. With phrases like these, and with manifestos in their back pockets, the hip young(ish) gunslingers of the oblique of the mid 1960s were making their mark.

Oblique spaces

Virilio had met a figure of some stature in Parent and the latter was initially the senior partner in the relationship. Claude Parent was by the early 1960s a noted and controversial figure in French architecture. He had become interested in 'architectural utopias' in the 1950s and did indeed go on to develop certain links with other 'utopists', but by the early 1960s he was becoming disillusioned with their kind of architectural thinking. Parent has recalled in interview that when the two of them met initially in 1963 Paul Virilio had no architectural training, and that 'when Virilio came to buy an apartment' in Paris 'he was a painter of stained glass'. Parent said that 'Virilio knew an extraordinary amount about his craft'. But Virilio 'also had a real instinct for architecture – an instinct reflected in his impulsive decision to buy that apartment', his old friend and colleague has remembered. In point of fact, Claude Parent was the architect of the apartment building! That real-estate 'moment' was how they originally paired up. Claude Parent and Paul Virilio subsequently began to collaborate on architectural projects in France in 1963 and carried on doing commissioned work until the late 1960s.

The painter of stained glass and the emerging architect proved to be a productive team. For instance, Virilio and Parent built the church of Sainte-Bernadette du Banlay in Nevers between 1964 and 1966. This was the pair's first practical project based on their unique 'function of the oblique' theory, which, as we have seen, had itself developed from ideas first generated by Virilio around 'bunker archaeology' and 'cryptic architecture'. The theory of the 'function of the oblique', which Virilio saw as the most important work of the Architecture Principe group, had its origins in the concepts of disequilibrium and motive instability. Accordingly, Virilio and Parent set the first structure to be built based on the theory of construction on an incline. The church of Sainte-Bernadette was a brutalist, menacing building deriving from the architecture inspired by the German bunkers, which Virilio had seen as themselves embodying an architecture of disequilibrium some years prior to this joint architectural venture. It symbolised much for the architectural duo. For the professional architect Claude Parent, it expressed 'our anger with the architecture and society of the time'. The three years' work on the church of Sainte-Bernadette and the completion of its construction preceded the development of the experimental theories in the *Architecture Principe* journal. Parent has recalled that the 'decision to apply this language' of the German bunkers 'to the form of the church came at a late stage in the project's development' so 'the formal references to bunkers should therefore be seen as a secondary element'. Paul Virilio, despite not being an architect and effectively 'hanging out' in his friend's office each day, was the one in the partnership who had the radical ideas, according to the later testimony of Parent. Virilio, he stated:

> had an admirable, and legitimate, ambition to make architecture and he contributed to the project in a very real way. It was Virilio who said that we should put a slope on the floor planes of the church ... The challenge of working together on a real, concrete project inspired a fundamental breakthrough – the first application of the function of the oblique. The military vocabulary of the bunkers dominated our early projects – the church as well as the cultural centre in Charleville. Virilio saw the bunker as the apotheosis of twentieth-century architecture. (Virilio and Parent 1996: 51)

The urban theorist and planner in Virilio was beginning to take shape. The military vocabulary of the German bunkers was always linked to the exploration of 'total war' and 'pure war' but it was also always connected to the city and the future of city planning for Virilio. Moreover, Virilio saw 'the city' as the 'result of war' or 'at least of preparation for war'. However, the first building venture illustrating the 'function of the oblique', despite being more or less achieved, did not exactly open the floodgates for the Virilio/Parent architectural partnership. Virilio had, as we have seen, prepared some stained-glass windows for churches and through this 'sacred art' link managed to secure the Sainte-Bernadette construction commission for himself and Parent. Further projects with Parent for a cultural centre in Charleville and a house in Saint-Germain-en-Laye were never actually built. The December 1966 issue (number 9) of *Architecture Principe* was entitled 'A Blueprint for Charleville' because that is exactly what it remained: a blueprint. But eventually another Parent/Virilio collaboration, namely the Thomson-Houston Aerospace Centre in Vélizy-Villacoublay, did come to fruition.

Theoretically the partnership of architectural ideas blossomed. In 1965 and 1966 Virilio and Parent presented papers to various conferences and seminars. Those given at Lyons, Locarno, Bologna and Lurs were collected together as the November 1966 issue (number 8) of *Architecture Principe*. The pair clearly collaborated personally, politically and theoretically in this period too, and not merely on the jointly authored magazine manifestos. For example,

in June 1966, at Folkestone across the Channel in England, they
were part of a panel on experimental architecture at a symposium
organised by the International Dialogue of Experimental Architecture (IDEA). The intervention by Parent and Virilio, a presentation
on 'oblique cities' delivered by the two Frenchmen dressed all in
black, bizarrely led to audience uproar still remembered thirty
years later by those present. The presentation was provocative, in
both form and content. If their intention was to provoke trouble in
England, the idea succeeded and they were duly booed off the stage
and given a Nazi or 'Hitlerian salute' by those they were addressing. Audience memory suggests that their choice of all-black
clothes (this was, after all, the year of the emergence in New York of
the Andy Warhol-influenced rock group the Velvet Underground)
rather than the psychedelic garb worn by other symposium
participants probably alienated the other architects present. But
the fact is that Parent and Virilio were not just disrupting the
conference by the way they looked: they were talking about the
futuristic possibility of 'oblique cities' all across the globe. Perhaps
the extent of the radicalism of Virilio and Parent in the context of
the architecture theory, and indeed practice, of the period should
not be forgotten. It is clear with the benefit of over three decades of
hindsight that the Folkestone incident symbolised the break they
had made with previous ideas. The 'horizontality' of the pre-indus-
trial era and the 'verticality' of the modernist, industrial epoch
were, for Parent and Virilio, to be transformed by the 'oblique' of
the post-industrial. Looking back, the fact that they were seen as
outsiders in 1966, and treated with suspicion and hostility, is hardly
surprising.

Architecturally the relationship would eventually come to a
close. The Thomson-Houston Aerospace project, assisted by Virilio's
good relationship with the engineer, turned out to be their final
completed collaboration. This came to an end in the period of 1968-9
because of a new project to construct a full-scale experimental
model of the 'function of the oblique'. The grandly named project,
'The Pendular Destabiliser no. 1', which Virilio and Parent intended
to inhabit for some weeks to test the equilibrium and habitability of
buildings on an incline, and to determine the best choice of angles
for the different living spaces, was in the process of being built at

the university of Nanterre in 1968. It was an experimental structure which was raised twelve metres from the ground to isolate it from the outside world. 'No telephone, no post, no means of communication – except for a little hole in the wall that we could talk to each other through' was how Parent recalled 'The Pendulum Destabiliser no. 1' as it was envisaged in its design. This 'psycho-physiological' experiment was curtailed not because of the impracticability of experimental living on inclined slopes, but because of wider political and cultural events in France. This just happened to be May 1968, and Nanterre's campus was where the spark was lit for the spectacular 'May '68' events in France, an upheaval which politically separated the previously close architectural colleagues.

May '68

In some ways May 1968 was the highpoint of Situationism, a creed with which Paul Virilio and Claude Parent were rather misleadingly associated by interpreters of their radical experimental architecture. In reality, Virilio and Parent were more comparable to figures like Jeremy Bentham in the nineteenth century who prepared an architectural plan of 'the Panopticon', an ingenious, not to mention oppressive, grand scheme for, as Bentham put it, 'grinding rogues honest', which was too ambitious in its architectural vision and was never actually built in the form in which it was conceived. The 'function of the oblique' can be compared in some senses to the Panopticon on these grounds. Its vision in theory was never properly realised in practice. Curiously, too, just as Bentham's design was described as his 'haunted house' and compared to the architecture and plan of management of the Gulags, Virilio and Parent's 'oblique spaces' were similarly 'compared to the prisons of the Bolshevik secret police, which had skewed cells and ceilings so low that it was impossible to stand'. Perhaps appropriately in view of the comparison of the two theorists separated by almost two centuries, Virilio uses the term 'panoptical' in his later work too and describes satellite and other electronic surveillance of the globe as if the whole world were now an electronic panopticon.

May 1968, with its students' and workers' uprisings and its riot police, saw the beginning of the end for the architectural partnership which had flourished for five or six years around the 'function of the oblique'. Situationism, and its effect on left-wing politics in France, was effectively at the centre of the disagreement between Paul Virilio and Claude Parent, a disagreement that ended their work together. Parent has remembered that he was 'upset that the political climate had so corrupted a friend of six years'. But other conflicts were surfacing too. For instance, both Virilio and Parent were anti-militarist but their critique of militarism was different and Parent has noted that Virilio 'did have a certain respect for the power of a collective organisation to achieve extraordinary, almost magical results that are beyond the power of the individual'. Parent also was 'not a practising Christian'. Perhaps most damningly, in 1968 Parent did not believe 'the function of the oblique' theory to have a 'political agenda'.

According to his later testimony looking back on the whole affair, the more conservative Parent plainly thought that the politics of 'May '68' were 'idiotic'. He has said that he did not even know what 'Situationist' meant at the time, whereas Virilio evidently threw himself into the 'spontaneous' situation with gusto. Parent has reminisced that:

> Virilio's experience of the time was very different. He was close to the hub of things. He wrote an article ... and he joined the group occupying the Odeon. When I went to see him, I was told that he was now calling himself 'Comrade Paul'. Those people all took themselves very seriously, forming 'revolutionary committees' and 'sub-committees'. I have no stomach for that kind of thing ... I don't like that mob mentality ... he was very much involved in the movement as a whole. He said it was something he'd been dreaming of all his life – 1789 revisited. All the same, he was no fool. The day the police stormed the Odeon and drove everyone out with their batons, he wasn't there. He'd gone home to take a bath. (Virilio and Parent 1996: 55)

Parent was right that as far as May 1968 is concerned, Paul Virilio 'was very much involved in the movement as a whole' although he was not in fact aligned with any group in particular. He has in interview expressed some sympathy for the 'Paris Commune', street resistance of an earlier era in his home city. He has noted, 'I feel rather close to the Communards, even if as a Christian I can't go along with their practice of slaughtering priests.' Furthermore, his assessment of Leon Trotsky was that he 'was a first-rate figure on matters of war'. Essentially, before and after May 1968, Virilio has consistently maintained a non-Marxist political stance. He has, however, on occasions shared something of the outlook of the ultra-leftist Italian Autonomist (or Autonomia) movement which sought to develop Marxism in a particular way in the modern world. For Virilio they 'failed in a Marxist perspective, according to which you have to change your life'. But the 'autonomists invented questions' and Virilio at the time responded to that, at least for a while. In any case Virilio believes, he has said, that 'only the movements which were able to cease, to stop by themselves before dropping dead' have really existed, and the Autonomists in his view managed to do that. Virilio has claimed not to 'believe in revolution' but in 'revolutionary resistance' and 'popular defence'. He has clearly pointed to the events of May 1968 as underlining his position at the time:

> I remember the speeches in the Richelieu Amphitheatre of the Sorbonne, before the taking of the Odeon Theatre at the very beginning of May '68. I went in: the place was packed. I heard a guy, probably a communist, say 'I read on the walls of the Sorbonne: "Imagination comes to power!" That's not true, it's the working class!' I answered: 'So, comrade, you deny the working class imagination.' It was pretty clear, one referring to a horde able to take power like a mass of soldiers, and the other (me) referring to the active imagination – the autonomists. On this level, at the time, I acted like them. (Virilio 1997a: 82)

So despite Parent's suspicion that Virilio was probably 'at the time much influenced by the Situationists', by his own admission it was the Autonomists who were more influential. As far as the Autonomists were in favour of 'the will to autonomy' as 'the will to get away from cultural and political conformity' Virilio has said that his work was in the same direction. Nevertheless, the Autonomists, particularly the Italian political scientist Toni Negri and others whom Semiotext(e), especially, went on to publish alongside Virilio in their various lists in the 1980s, differed considerably in practical political activity in the 1970s compared with anything Virilio became involved with in the context of the events of May 1968. In any case, as Parent recalled many years later, Paul Virilio always 'was a great reader' and his reading included all kinds of social and cultural analysis, from the the Situationists and Autonomists at one end of the spectrum to the likes of J. K. Galbraith at the other. He very much went with the flow of May 1968, as many others did without holding for evermore to its political roots. Whatever the precise cause of the political split which meant that they could no longer work together, 1968–9 was effectively the end for Virilio and Parent, and to a large extent the architectural movement they had founded.

Although 'May '68' symbolically put an end to the partnership – theoretical and practical – of Paul Virilio and Claude Parent, the outriders of 'architecture beginning again' did continue for a while, although independently of each other, with some further development of the ideas surrounding the theory of 'the function of the oblique'. Parent, for instance, continued to explore 'the oblique' in a whole series of practical architectural projects, designing an oblique house in 1969, an oblique pavilion in 1970 and several other urban projects in the 1970s. As for Virilio, he has emphasised that:

> After I became co-director of the Ecole Spéciale d'Architecture in Paris in 1972, my teaching concentrated on the development of technical research into the organisation and the precise morphology of oblique volumes. Several student theses were devoted to this theme, but after a few years the overwhelming difficulties of building an oblique habitat led us to abandon this work which seemed to offer no practical benefit to young architects starting out in the working world. (Virilio and Parent 1996: 13)

The pair of architectural radicals whom the French architectural press of the 1960s had misleadingly labelled 'post-Corbusians' had finally given in to the more prosaic demands of the 1970s. In the context of the Architecture Principe group, Parent and Virilio's work was seen to 'subvert modernism's quest for stable foundations', and the two of them in harness put into practice Virilio's idea of a 'negative, critical aesthetic' where the 'vocabulary of the bunker was intended to create a repellent architecture that would overrun established perceptions and provoke a response from the user, in the same spirit as the Situationists'. 'Situationism' and even 'anarchism' may have been some of the rather excessive post-hoc labelling and interpretation of Paul Virilio's behaviour and political and cultural stance in May 1968, and there is no doubt that the older and more cautious Parent perceived such tendencies at the time in the actions of Virilio. Nevertheless, within a year Virilio had been nominated as a professor, and a more respectable future, one of training 'young architects starting out in the working world', beckoned as the euphoria of the late 1960s faded across the globe, especially in Virilio's home country of France. 'Consumer society' was to proliferate with a vengeance after 1968. Virilio has spoken little about 'May '68' in interviews since that time but looking back in the early 1980s with Sylvère Lotringer he recalled that:

> All of '68 was against the consumer society. All the youth movements (there are many names for them) at the end of the 60s in the West were, to my mind, signs of the danger of gluttonous consumption. The exaggeration of consumption was pointing toward something fearsome, even though it remained diffused. Not that the students themselves (most of whom were middle class) had been against a relative development of consumption: but they understood that its excesses were leading towards collapse. In this consumption beyond all limits, there was a proliferation of collapse and of Western civilian society's nondevelopment. (Virilio 1997a: 151)

After '68

Remembering Paul Virilio's 1950s and 1960s past is more than just a useful exercise in excavation of biographical details, although it is most certainly that too, because it helps to set Virilio in context in a way not achieved in previous writings about him. Most considerations of Virilio's life and work to date have not had much to say about Paul Virilio in the 1950s and 1960s, and where that period is mentioned, it is almost in footnote form as if the 1970s and beyond were where Virilio's work really started. There has been little attempt to provide the kind of chronology set out here and even less suggestion that from the 1950s and 1960s we can see more clearly where Virilio's trajectory has been and where it has been going ever since. The partnership of Virilio and Parent, although it did not endure, was a formative period in his life and work. After the five-year collaboration with Parent, interestingly, Virilio mainly worked alone. A new phase would, however, open up, one which would spawn many books and essays. Virilio the international writer and intellectual was about to be created. In 1969, Paul Virilio has recalled, he began writing the first chapters of a book he was to publish in full several years later as *L'Insécurité du Territoire* (Virilio 1993b).

For the newly politically enthused Virilio, nothing would be the same again after 1968, although his global reputation took a long time to be fully established. Made Professor of the Ecole Spéciale d'Architecture in Paris in 1969, he became its co-director with Anatole Kopp in 1972, its full director in 1975 and eventually its President in 1990, leaving in 1999 with the title Emeritus Professor. Alhough Architecture Principe no longer existed as a group and a magazine/journal after his serious falling-out with Parent (apart from the return in 1996 when they produced the special thirtieth anniversary issue, number 10), Virilio's place as a public intellectual in France meant that he was asked to be on the editorial boards of a number of journals as well as to contribute articles on a range of subjects over the next thirty years. Virilio actively participated in the running of ventures such as the journal *Critiques*, the progressive Christian magazine *Esprit*, the leftist journal *Cause Commune*, and the magazine of the Pompidou Centre *Traverses*, which he edited with Jean Baudrillard (with whom he is often misleadingly bracketed in a more general political and theoretical sense). *La Pourissement des Sociétés*, a collection of extracts from the pages of *Cause Commune* between 1972 and 1974, was produced by an editorial team including Paul Virilio and the sociologist and writer Georges Perec in 1975.

By the mid 1970s the world that Virilio had begun to view afresh in the 1950s and 1960s was upon us. What the media labelled as 'terrorism' and Virilio had already started to call 'state terrorism' or 'interstate delinquencies' was by then gathering pace and changing Virilio's focus. In 1975 the first edition of Virilio's first book, the French language *Bunker Archéologie*, was published. In this period, once again with the help of Georges Perec, Virilio created the 'Collection L'Espace Critique' at the Paris publishers Galilée and edited the series from 1973. Much of Paul Virilio's book output in French since 1977 has been in this well-known imprint with its famous cool, supposedly 'sexy', modernist, cream 'hard' book covers, red title lettering and black author names. Some of Virilio's intellectual friends in Paris, such as Jean Baudrillard and Félix Guattari (with whom he founded the free radio station Radio Tomate in 1979), regularly had their books published in the 'Espace Critique' series in the 1980s and 1990s. Some of these books found their English translations as Semiotext(e) 'little black books' out of New York, as Virilio's have done. In Virilio's case most English readers have only seen his writing in this American format and never in the elegant design of Galilée's 'Collection L'Espace Critique', which seems to scream 'Danger, serious intellectual at work', and ends up in sections labelled 'brainy stuff' in the independent bookshops of the world.

Intellectual imposture?

To the extent that Virilio is taken seriously by an English-speaking audience, and not ridiculed along with other 'French theory', there has also been strong reaction to his work. In the twenty-first-century English-speaking world Virilio is regarded, and remembered, mainly as the 'high priest of speed'. But Paul Virilio is not only this. More generally he is seen as one of France's leading contemporary intellectuals and in the last few years his large body of work has started to be discussed throughout the world. The French media have called him 'one of the most original thinkers of our time'. He is certainly one of the most noted French theorists of contemporary culture and has been so for more than thirty years. He has been a city planner, urbanist, architectural theorist, homelessness campaigner, art curator, film critic, museum exhibitor, military historian, free radio activist and peace strategist, among many other roles. He was founding member of the Centre for Interdisciplinary Research in Peace Studies and Military Strategy (CIRPES) and later joined Alain Joxe's Sociology of Defense group at the Ecole des Hautes Etudes en Sciences Sociales in Paris. In 1990 he became programme director at the Collège International de Philosophie headed by Jacques Derrida. Paul Virilio has been described as a 'brilliant, complex and wonderfully idiosyncratic thinker', 'one of the leading French theorists addressing late twentieth-century media culture' and, perhaps most aptly, 'the emblematic French theorist of technology'. At the same time, in some of the most vitriolic criticism of his work, Paul Virilio has been labelled 'post-science' or 'science friction' and a representative of 'unthinkingness'.

Most notoriously, the natural-science-based 'prankster' duo Alan Sokal and Jean Bricmont devoted a short chapter to Virilio in their poorly conceived *Intellectual Impostures* (Sokal and Bricmont 1999), a book-length critique of French theorists of what they call 'postmodernism' in general and 'philosophical' writers like Paul Virilio in particular. In the course of a supposed wholesale demolition of what they mistakenly call 'postmodern philosophers' abuse of science', the writing of Paul Virilio was labelled 'pseudo-scientific verbiage' and 'diarrhoea of the pen'. The essence of their critique – of the other theorists attacked in the book as much as of Virilio alone – was the French postmodern philosopher's alleged failure to understand the elementary physics with which the writing is often peppered. In fact, as Virilio has asserted in interview, he does actually 'have a formal scientific education' which is 'why physics and military sciences kept' him 'busy for a long time'. This, in Virilio's estimation, is in sharp contrast to, for instance, Jean Baudrillard, another of Sokal and Bricmont's hate-figures. Unlike Baudrillard, Paul Virilio can claim to be able 'to take a detour through physics'. In the 'intellectual impostures' chapter on him written by Sokal and Bricmont, Virilio was specifically singled out for, among other sins, confusing 'acceleration' (the rate of change of velocity) with 'speed', as well as the allegedly poor quality of much of the language of the English translation of his work. However, if we are serious about getting to the bottom of the significance, or otherwise, of the long life and work of Paul Virilio, it is actually to poetics not physics that we should look for an intelligent guide to Virilio – what Sean Cubitt (Cubitt 2001) has called, in relation to Jean Baudrillard as well as Paul Virilio, the 'poetics of pessimism'. This present book endorses such a cultural approach to French theory, including that of Virilio. Whether it pins down Virilio categorically is questionable. Virilio himself has agreed that he paints 'a dark picture because few are willing to do it', although he does not actually wear the badge of 'pessimist' too

well. The question for him surrounds the issue of belief, or otherwise, in technological progress:

> The same idealism that caused the catastrophes and the ravages of the twentieth century is resurfacing today. I am definitely not against progress, but after the ecological and ethical catastrophes we have seen, not only Auschwitz but also Hiroshima, it would be unforgiveable to allow ourselves to be deceived by the kind of utopia which insinuates that technology will ultimately bring about happiness and a greater sense of humanity. (Virilio 1999: 79)

By no means does this book give a wholesale endorsement of Paul Virilio's work, and there are many important reservations to be entered about his positions. However, unfortunately for Sokal and Bricmont, these reservations are not registered in the 'intellectual impostures' critique.

Reading Virilio

In the context of the Sokal and Bricmont text, our scientific heroes' attention to the actual writing of Paul Virilio, as opposed to mistranslations or the myriad (mis)uses and misinterpretations of Virilio in all kinds of disciplines, is an important lesson. Accordingly, this present book seeks to 'read' the texts of Virilio, in French and English translation, and not to rely on what we might like to think Paul Virilio has said and written over the years. There is no substitute for reading, and re-reading, Virilio. He is an important, innovative contemporary cultural thinker and he will be read and interpreted long after his own death.

The task of reading Virilio has been made easier by the fact that much of his French-language writing is now available in English translation. This is thanks especially to the Semiotext(e) editors Jim Fleming and Sylvère Lotringer (and various translators) at Columbia University, New York, who have published English editions of Virilio's work in their 'little black books' – both 'Double Agents' and 'Foreign Agents' series – and in single-issue volumes. Verso, Sage and University of Minnesota Press, among other publishers, have put out various texts in English and extended the interest in Virilio's four decades of commentating on many diverse topics. In addition, a number of significant interviews are available in

English translation in which Virilio looks back on his earlier work, muses on world events and comments on his contemporary writings. Paul Virilio's work, although becoming much more available than hitherto in the international academy and beyond, is pervasive in influence but as yet, even if properly acknowledged, relatively poorly understood, and there is only a relatively limited literature on Virilio. This is partly because until recently the entire back catalogue of his work was difficult to obtain. However, that can no longer be used as such an easy excuse when reading and using Virilio. Still, what seem to be wilful misinterpretations persist. One of his most straightforward and readable works, *Strategy of Deception* (2000a), a book about military intervention and justice in the highly accelerated and sometimes dangerous modern world, was reviewed not long ago in a serious English newspaper by a writer (let us leave him or her nameless) who thought:

> One wouldn't want to eat an entire plate of ripe Camembert every day although it's a nice occasional treat. Similarly with the ultra-French conceptualist Virilio. Here he is again with a small but fierce volume about NATO's war in the Balkans ... You too can make Virilio at home: mix equal parts Foucault, Baudrillard and Chomsky, add eight cloves of garlic and blow up with two sticks of dynamite. Then start typing.

Sadly for this critic, Paul Virilio is really nothing like Michel Foucault, Jean Baudrillard and Noam Chomsky, however they are mixed. In the pages of this book such comparisons with Virilio's intellectual peers are questioned, and detailed scrutiny of Virilio's thinking and writing is undertaken alongside other such thinkers of the twentieth- and twenty-first centuries. As this book makes abundantly clear, there are reasons why it might be good to 'forget' Virilio as we have learnt to forget Foucault (at Jean Baudrillard's insistence) and to forget Baudrillard (at his own insistence). But there are also many reasons why we should remember Virilio too.

CHAPTER TWO

Accelerated modernity

Paul Virilio is best known as a theorist of speed even to the casual observer of his work today. As we have seen in the book so far, critics call him the 'high priest of speed', and he almost revels in the label, claiming he has introduced us to a totally new world which has never been shown before, since 'not many writers have touched on speed'. Although this is not all that Virilio's work comprises, as this book shows, it is still an important and pervasive aspect. He has added the speed dimension to all kinds of different analyses in which it did not feature previously: speed and vision, speed and war, speed and technology, speed and politics, speed and space-time, and so on. Certainly, in Virilio's world-view, the 'question of war' is 'summed up in the question of speed, of its organisation and production, in short of everything that surrounded it'. In this chapter we shall introduce the term 'accelerated modernity' to help to frame the contribution of Virilio on speed.

It has been argued by certain sympathetic observers that Virilio's 'fascination with technologies of speed and vision' warrants his body of work being assessed as highly as, for example, his fellow countryman Michel Foucault's books such as *Birth of the Clinic*, *Madness and Civilisation*, *Discipline and Punish* or *History of Sexuality*. It has even been argued that Virilio is 'successor, debtor and faithful disciple' of Michel Foucault (Douglas 1996). There is reason to disagree with this contention. Virilio's analyses are, quite simply, of a very different order to those of Foucault. In the words of one critic who has compared them, 'Virilio is a dromologist, not an historian'. Even though Virilio might be seen as a 'genealogist of motion', as Foucault has been described as a genealogist of power, the dromological society is not the same as disciplinary society. In any case Paul Virilio has stated quite clearly in interview: 'I respect Michel Foucault more than I like him.' Moreover, the aim of the whole writing and researching project is, for Virilio, a different outcome. Not for him the in-depth and detailed historical explanation of the prison, the teaching hospital, the asylum or sexuality. As Virilio has acknowledged, 'I don't believe in explanations. I believe in suggestions, in the obvious quality of the implicit.' Consequently, in contrast to the great tomes of Michel Foucault and others, Paul Virilio has set out bold, key thinking in some very pithy books, but as he himself has noted 'it's not the amount of pages that count'. He has claimed to 'never write long things' and seems proud that his books 'don't last very long'.

The body in movement

Paul Virilio's work has always had a 'speed' dimension to it. Even the 'bunker archaeology' originally emerging in the 1950s and the long 'cryptic architecture' collaboration with Claude Parent in the 1960s were based around movement. As we have noted already, the Architecture Principe group manifestos rejected the traditional axes of the horizontal and the vertical. The 'function of the oblique' employed oblique planes to create an architecture of disequilibrium in an attempt to bring the habitat into a dynamic era of the body in movement – 'habitable circulation' as Virilio has called it. The 'body in movement' has remained a focus for Virilio's theorising ever since. Virilio has said that the body was 'extremely important to me', a 'planet', a 'universe' which 'technology is invading …. because of miniaturisation'. This process is everywhere for Virilio, whether in transport or transplants:

> Miniaturisation is a dwarfing effect that concerns both the medium and its object. The new transportation technologies – the Concorde, supersonic planes, the high-speed train – reduce and miniaturise the distances of the territorial body, in other words of the environment. The miniaturisation of technical objects, known as nanotechnologies, is the ability to create micromachines capable of merging with our organs. This technology will not miniaturise the human body, but rather its properties. It will reduce the properties of the living under the pretext of completing and assisting them. (Virilio 1999: 55)

The concept of the body in Virilio's work is, then, the result of 'not simply the combination of dance, muscles, body-building, strength and sex'. But, to continue the comparison of Virilio and Foucault, it is most certainly not the 'produced' body of Michel Foucault's power/knowledge discourses, either. Foucault conceives of 'docile bodies' being produced and regulated through the birth of the prison and criminology in the eighteenth and nineteenth centuries, and further the sexualised body in the 'incitement to discourse' he finds in the long history of sexuality from Greek and

Roman times onwards. Virilio not only relies on the quality of the implicitness and suggestiveness he finds in all kinds of anecdotal snippets of evidence in military history about the body; he conceives of it as 'pre-existing' history. The body in Virilio comes first; dancing is before writing. The body in Virilio is *a priori*. Moreover, he has said that in his thinking there are:

> three bodies that are eminently connected: the territorial body, that of the planet and ecology; the social body; and finally the animal or human body. From this results the need to reorient oneself with respect to the body with respect to the other – the question of the neighbour and alterity – but also with respect to the Earth, or the world proper. There cannot be a body proper without a world proper, without a proper orientation. The body proper is oriented with respect to the other, whether woman, friend, enemy ... but it is also oriented with respect to the world proper. It is 'here and now' ... Being is present here and now. (Virilio 1999: 43–4)

To Claude Parent's mind, too, the body in motion was present from the very beginning of Virilio's work. The motion of the bunkers, strange as it may seem, was the jumping-off point. As Parent has argued, 'some bunkers also have a sense of movement. If you look at them for long enough, they seem to be advancing towards you – like tanks.'

Acknowledging the effects of this movement in military space, Virilio has labelled his own nostalgic discourse on the original Architecture Principe group work, from the standpoint of the mid 1990s retrospective collection, as 'Disorientation'. Virilio has recalled the origins of this idea in his introduction to the French and English versions of all ten of the manifestos, written in 1996:

> Prohibited and castigated by the advocates, today consigned to oblivion of historical materialism, the Architecture Principe group was to rapidly disappear at the dawn of that postmodern syncretism whose misdeeds would clutter the decade of the 70s before a few architects worthy of the name finally appeared, in France and elsewhere ... Here was our project: starting from the moving body, to make full use of gravity's energy in the three temporal dimensions of physical movement, taking advantage in quite a Galilean way of the surface of inclined planes in order to achieve truly habitable circulation opposed to the habitable fixity of the classic

apartment building. Thus there was, at the origin of the theory of our group, the idea of disequilibrium and motor instability. The idea that gravity, terrestrial gravitation, is a motor to be used like the wind in the sails of a ship; hence the implementation of inclined supports and the use of horizontality as a 'threshold of balance' between two inclined surfaces ... what was ... fiercely contested and called into question was the postural schema of the classical age, the reference to the essentially static and stationary proprioception of the sedentary body. This contestation was aimed at bringing at last the human habitat into the era of the dynamics of bodies in movement. (Virilio and Parent 1997: 7–9)

Aside from making clear his views on postmodern architecture's 'misdeeds' in the 1970s, from the relative safety of the 1990s, and offering a retort to those who label him a postmodernist (a debate which we shall consider later in the book), Virilio's look back at the Architecture Principe pointed forward to an era beyond contemporary modernity. In that era, as he has elsewhere admitted, the human body might 'disappear', even if 'we haven't reached that point yet'. There is certainly a 'dictatorship of movement' occurring for Virilio with new forms of sedentariness. Where the 'airport today has become the new city', there is what he calls 'polar inertia' in the blur of movement:

> When a businessman travels from Paris to New York, New York–Paris, Paris–New York, New York–Paris by Concorde, he begins to experience the situation of polar inertia. This new form of sedentariness is the active tendency in technology. Sedentariness in the instant of absolute speed. It's no longer a sedentariness of non-movement, it's the opposite ... The sedentaries of transportation are very simply travellers who buy a plane ticket at Roissy-en-France at Orly – for Roissy or Orly. They go around the world as fast as possible without going anywhere, barely making the necessary refuelling stop, and nothing else. An empty voyage, a voyage without destination, a circular voyage, which puts immediacy to the test ... I think it's a form of desire for inertia, desire for ubiquity, instantaneousness. (Virilio 1997a: 69)

The whole area of genetics, as well as transportation, affects the body in Virilio's work, too. Today, in Virilio's account, 'the body simulates the relationship to the world' as the 'colonisation of the human body by technology' continues apace, through tiny implants.

Transplants for Virilio constitute the third technological revolution after transportation and electronic communications and may lead to what Celia Lury (1998) has described as a more widespread 'prosthetic culture'. According to Virilio, 'we started with human implants, but research leads us to microtechnological implants'. He has labelled himself as 'a materialist of the body' viewing the body as 'fundamental' and 'all technologies' as invading the body, but the reader of Virilio cannot help feeling that the religious faith he holds dear determines the conceptualisation of the body in his work. Even if he does not declare the body to be sacred as such, there is a sense of paranoia and claustrophobia surrounding its technological colonisation in Virilio's comments. For Virilio, 'technology now aspires to occupy the body'. The body itself is the 'last remaining territory'. 'Domotics' and the 'smart house' of the future governed by electronic gadgets reveal for him that the idea of the body in motion might be at an end. New technologies for Virilio make human habitation possible without movement. Virilio has noted in interview with Philippe Petit that:

> the question of domotics is related to both the question of inhabited space or the habitation – 'house', 'dwelling' – and that of the relation to the body of the inhabitant ... The human body is the reference for its habitat. The ergonomic dimension of the body must be taken into consideration in the habitat. However the new technologies make habitation possible without moving. With domotics, it's not television channels that are zapped but rather the lights, the heat and the opening of the shutters. You don't have to go to the window to open it, just zap it. So there is a kind of reference to a handicapped body and no longer to a locomotive body. The over-equipped able-body of domotics, the one that experiences home automation, is the equivalent of the equipped invalid. (Virilio 1999: 66)

So polar inertia is reached. Virilio has cited the millionaire recluse Howard Hughes as the man who 'lived to the limit of polar inertia'. Hughes had 'a hand in everything that appeared at that time having to do with speed, the airplane and the cinema', living 'polar inertia' by 'having several apartments all over the world, each decorated the same way'. Daily he was 'served the same meal, brought the same paper at the same times, taking into account the differences in time-zone'. Hughes, to Virilio's mind, 'lived inertia', surviving the last fifteen years of his life shut up in a hotel watching the same films without getting out of bed. However, all of this, from Virilio's perspective on technological change, depends on speed: Hughes, according to Virilio, owed his power to speed. Now, however, with polar inertia more generalised, everyone can be driven mad by the sedentariness brought on by the quest for speed.

Speed politics

For Virilio, for the world 'to have reached the speed of light, is an historical event which throws history in disarray and jumbles up the relation of the living being towards the world'. Speed, and particularly the speed of light, is fundamental to an explanation of how global society works today as far as he is concerned. Virilio has argued that 'global society is currently in a gestation period and cannot be understood without the speed of light or the automatic quotations of the stock market in Wall Street, Tokyo or London'. The speed of war and the speed of communication (in the sense of the radio, including Radio Free France in the Second World War, which was so important to the organisation of resistance to the German occupation) were of course early childhood memories for Virilio and the twin foci, war and communication, never seem to leave his vision.

It could even be said that speed and movement have been increasingly at the centre of Virilio's interests as the years passed from childhood into early adulthood and beyond. Perhaps inevitably, a politics of speed has developed which was not always formally present in the earlier forays into the body in movement. Although, as we have seen, Virilio fell out with Claude Parent over the latter not giving enough political resonance to the theory of the 'function of the oblique', a speed politics only really emerged later. Readers of Virilio's post-'May '68' writings can witness the way Virilio has constantly, but diversely, illuminated the politicisation of speed in contemporary culture. For Virilio's work to function, speed is so central it is political. Speed, he has said, 'is power itself'. Further, according to Virilio in typically declaratory mode, 'power and speed are inseparable, just as wealth and speed are inseparable':

The question of speed is central. It pertains to the question of economy. Not only is speed a threat, insofar as it is capitalised and tyrannical, but it is also life itself. Speed and wealth go hand in hand. To give a philosophical definition of speed we can say that it is not a phenomenon, but rather the relationship between phenomena. In other words it is relativity itself. We can go even further and say that speed is a milieu. It doesn't just involve the time between two points, but a milieu that is provoked by a vehicle … for me, speed is my milieu. (Virilio 1999: 14)

In the perhaps perverse and confusing view of some commentators, speed produces culture, not the other way round, and while his argument is certainly not reducible to this format, Virilio has been at the forefront of the arguments over such aspects of technology and modernity. Sometimes, however, his formulations in this regard are rather crude and deterministic. He has talked, for instance, about 'speed classes':

In the nineteenth century, it was thought that the railroad would create a world democracy and reunite the peoples of Europe into one single agora. The idea was that the railroads would favour conviviality and solidarity. Let me remind you that there were seaside trains or express trains that were very expensive and didn't go very far, from Paris to Deauville, for example; thus there would be first, second and third classes. There we have real 'speed classes'. You have to take the express, whereas the slow train is reserved for the poorest people … every time there is progress in speed, we are told: democracy will follow; yet we know very well that this is not the case … There is the illusion of redemptory speed, the illusion that bringing populations together in the most extreme way will not bring about conflicts but love, that one must love one's distant neighbour as oneself. (Virilio 1999: 19)

Virilio has furthermore argued for speed to be seen as the primary characteristic of knowledge and for space and time to be seen as the products of speed. One of his most pervasive connections has been speed and vision, or more appropriately speed and the 'vision machine', so evident in contemporary warfare as more and more cruise missiles and unmanned drones darken the world's skies. The progress of speed and the image of the world that we create for ourselves are inextricable for Virilio:

Speed enables you to see. It does not simply allow you to arrive at your destination more quickly, rather it enables you to see and foresee. To see, yesterday with photography and cinema, and to foresee today with electronics, the calculator and the computer. Speed changes the world vision. In the nineteenth century, with photography and cinema, world vision became 'objective' ... It can be said that today, vision is becoming 'teleobjective'. That is to say that television and multimedia are collapsing the close shots of time and space as a photograph collapses the horizon in the telephotographic lens. Thus speed enables you to see differently, and it is beginning with the nineteenth century that this world vision changes and public space becomes a public image through photography, cinematography and television. (Virilio 1999: 21)

Speed and ways of seeing like the cinema are thus not confined in Virilio to references to films like *Speed* and *Speed 2*, directed by Jan de Bont, although Virilio does in fact cite them as an example of what he calls a 'cinema of acceleration', and he has himself been cited approvingly by film theorists as helping to theorise a cinema of 'derealisation' (Telotte 1999). Speed, in Virilio's phenomenological vista, is an integral part of a world vision or 'world perception' where the world becomes cinematic.

Crucially, however, the same phenomena of speed and contemporary culture are different today in Virilio's view than they were when he first started writing about them in any sustained manner in the 1970s and 1980s. He contemplated this change in an interview with Carlos Oliveira in the mid 1990s where he related the issue to the general arguments he has been making for a decade or more about the consequences of 'accelerated temporality' or the 'acceleration of our daily lives':

This is because we are witnessing a radical break; it is not my thinking that has become radical, the situation itself has radicalised beyond measure. The end of the bloc-oriented confrontation between East and West, the transition from the industrial to the INFORMATIONAL mode of production, the globalisation that is being achieved through the telecommunication networks and the information (super)highways – all these developments raise grave questions. (1995)

Even though some of the language and rhetoric recall the same

mode of thinking and conceptualisation, Virilio has moved beyond
the writings of neo-Marxism, in the work of Mark Poster and
others, on the 'mode of information' and introduced a speed politics
into the equation through the notion of the 'accident'. The 'accident', in Virilio's use and specialised terminology, is a complicated
and ambiguous notion. Here, as frequently happens elsewhere in
Virilio's oeuvre, the English translation oversimplifies by connoting
merely a catastrophic event rather than the deeper philosophical
reference to 'accidence and substance' and the phenomenological
debates Virilio inherited from those he listened to at the Sorbonne
in the 1960s. Virilio, for his part, has argued that,

> For the philosopher substance is absolute and necessary, whereas
> the accident is relative and contingent. So the accident is what
> happens unexpectedly to the substance, the product or the recently
> invented technical object. It is for example the original accident of
> the Challenger space shuttle ten years ago. It is the duty of scientists
> and technicians to avoid the accident at all costs ... In fact, if no
> substance can exist in the absence of an accident, then no technical
> object can be developed without in turn generating 'its' specific
> accident: ship=ship wreck, train=train wreck, plane=plane crash,
> etc. The accident is thus the hidden face of technical progress ...
> one thing that must be considered here is the preponderance and
> role of the speed of the accident, thus the limitation of speed and
> the penalties for 'exceeding the speed limit'. With the acceleration
> following the transportation revolution of the last century, the
> number of accidents suddenly multiplied and sophisticated pro-
> cedures had to be invented in order to control air, rail and highway
> traffic. With the current world-wide revolution in communication
> and telematics, acceleration has reached its physical limit, the speed
> of electromagnetic waves. So there is a risk not of a local accident in
> a particular location, but rather of a global accident that would
> affect if not the entire planet, then at least the majority of people
> concerned by these technologies ... It is apparent that this new
> notion of the accident has nothing to do with the Apocalypse, but
> rather with the imperious necessity to anticipate in a rational way
> this kind of catastrophe by which the interactivity of tele-
> communications would reproduce the devastating effects of a
> poorly managed radioactivity – think about Chernobyl. (Virilio
> 1999: 92–3)

The nature of the 'accident', which we shall consider in more specific detail and case study later in this book, has changed, according to Virilio, and changed speed and everything else in its wake, as he told Carlos Oliveira in interview:

> The information revolution which we are currently witnessing ushers in the era of the global accident. The old kind of accidents were localised in space and time: a train derailment took place, say, in Paris or in Berlin; and when a plane crashed, it did so in London or wherever in the world. The catastrophes of earlier time were situated in real space, but now, with the advent of absolute speed of light and electromagnetic waves, the possibility of a global accident has arisen, of an accident that would occur simultaneously to the world as a whole. (1995)

Despite the fact that the information revolution has not had a great deal of effect on Virilio himself – he uses the internet only rarely, he has at times almost given up watching television – he has said that he does regard 'cyberspace as a new form of perspective'. Through 'cyberspace' especially (Virilio 1995b), for Virilio, history 'has just struck the wall of world-wide time' where with 'live transmission, local time no longer creates history', where 'real time conquers real space', producing a 'time accident, an accident with no equal', as he told David Dufresne (1996) in an interview. According to Virilio, in interview with Oliveira, 'speeding up' has meant reaching the limit of speed, that of 'real time':

> A possible symptom of this globalisation, of the eventuality of such an accident, was the stock exchange crash of 1987. We will no longer live in local time as we did in the past when we were prisoners of history. We will live in world time, in global time. We are experiencing an epoch that spells the international, the global accident. This is the way I interpret simultaneity and its imposition upon us, as well as the immediacy and the ubiquity, that is, the omnipresence of the information bomb, which at the moment, thanks to the information (super)highways and all the technological breakthroughs and developments in the field of telecommunication, is just about to explode. (1995)

The society of the accident, which Virilio foresees in his discussion with Carlos Oliveira, is the subject of much of his thinking in the late 1990s and into the twenty-first century and has all kinds of implications, but what is noteworthy in this clear statement of his theoretical argument (with all its flaws and possibilities) is that speed has its political consequences. Indeed, Virilio has insisted that we must 'politicise speed', whether it be 'metabolic speed (the speed of the living being, of reflexes) or technological speed', because, in his view 'speed is just as important as wealth in founding politics' in pre-modernity and modernity.

Accelerated culture

'Modernity' as a concept is undergoing an enormous renaissance in global theorising in the humanities and social sciences as a political position which accepts capitalism – or capitalisms – as the high-point of human existence, displacing the Marxist notion of socialism. Moreover, communism, *following* capitalism, has gained dominance. Unlike other recent theorisations of modernity – such as Ulrich Beck's 'second modernity', Zygmunt Bauman's 'liquid modernity' and various notions of 'hypermodernity' (which has in fact been linked with Paul Virilio through the arguments associated with the work of John Armitage), not to mention the concep-tualisation of the global network society by Manuel Castells – Paul Virilio has never been unequivocally a theorist of 'late modernity', although he has always brought a high modernist stance to this particular end-of-the-century party. However, it is arguable that Virilio's work fits best into what has been elsewhere called the theorisation of an accelerated culture, or, better still, what we might now call in the context of this book 'accelerated modernity'.

Is this twenty-first-century modernity, then, the 'age of the accelerator' (replacing the 'age of the brake') where Paul Virilio is a theorist whose time has come at last? This book is a partial answer to such a question and it is important to continue to pursue it. Certainly it is from this aspect of Virilio's concerns that he has been a self-labelled 'dromologist', analysing the 'dromological revolu-tion' and 'dromoscopy' and producing 'dromologies' (Wilbur 1994). This has been his venture in fact for more than thirty years. Virilio himself has given a neat working definition of 'dromology' as:

the diverse phenomena of acceleration in this era of the 'global village'. The focus of my research has shifted from TOPOLOGY to DROMOLOGY i.e. the study and analysis of the impact of the increasing speed of transport and communications. (Virilio and Parent 1996: 13)

As Virilio has directly pointed out, linguistically the concept of 'dromology' comes originally from the Greek 'dromos', which simply means race. But the possible application of the concept and its theoretical framework takes us into quite different realms. His friend Jean Baudrillard has acknowledged the significance of Virilio's dromology in understanding an event like, say, 'May '68', which, as Sylvère Lotringer has suggested to Baudrillard in interview, 'outraced everybody'. Baudrillard's answer to Lotringer was succinct and clear:

> When the effect goes faster and faster than the cause, it devours it. I could easily see the 'speed-up' analysed by Paul Virilio from this angle, as an attempt to accelerate faster than linearity can handle. Speed is different from movement. Movement goes somewhere, speed nowhere. (Genosko 2001: 123)

Indeed, Jean Baudrillard has gone on to claim, without specifically citing Virilio as an influence although he is clearly present in the background, that 'things have become so accelerated that processes are no longer inscribed in a linear temporality, in a linear unfolding of history'. This in fact is an interesting, if typically idiosyncratic, even 'Baudrillardian', retrospective interpretation of Virilio's contribution to theorising modernity by means of 'dromology' and can be seen as a constant overriding theme of this book. It may not be the realm of movement as such where Virilio contributes so much to our understanding if we are to heed Baudrillard. It is, moreover, in pursuing the Baudrillard line on linear temporality and linear history that the sphere, or domain, of accelerated culture is brought into view in Virilio's long trajectory since May 1968 as dromologist, cultural theorist, architectural teacher and urban planner. It is possible to claim that Virilio is a theorist for an accelerated culture as a whole rather than merely the speeding-up of military technology. Popular culture, which is characterised not by content (which creative or cultural industry fits within its boundaries, or which art form) but increasingly by the speed with which its products become outdated, and recycled, or by the speed with which the underground becomes overground (and vice versa), is one contemporary example of accelerated culture.

What might be the main characteristic of such an accelerated culture then, and when historically did it emerge, according to those who make theoretical claims for it? This subject is wide enough for a book-length answer of its own. But it can be argued cogently here, in the context of Virilio's life and work, that accelerated culture in so far as it impinges on Virilio's explorations dates from the Second World War. That conflict has so often been Virilio's historical starting-point, particularly in terms of the scale of its violence, the speeding-up of its military technology and the long shadow it cast over the subsequent fifty years, especially in a country like France. Virilio has said in interview with Nicholas Zurbrugg that he has always seen the whole of the twentieth century as 'a century of hyper-violence':

> For me, the century that I've experienced – the twentieth century – is a century of hyper-violence in all domains. In the domain of war – Auschwitz and Hiroshima, in the domain of technology – the extraordinary power of the technology allowing landings on the moon, but also Chernobyl … The climate of the twentieth century is not confused at all. It is as brutal as a fist in the face. For me, my century is the century of horror. Not simply a century of terror, but of horror … So for me, there is no confusion – it's a very violent century. One might say that it is the century of war. (1996a: 112)

The Australian historian Richard Bosworth, in the process of theorising what he sees as the short and long Second World War in his book about explaining Auschwitz and Hiroshima (Bosworth 1993), has stressed the effect on France and French culture through to the end of the twentieth century. Bosworth's argument – that there are long and short Second World Wars and that France had a 'short' Second World War between 1939 and 1940 but proceeded to 'fight' the 'long' Second World War through culture in the rest of the postwar years – helps us to situate the perspective of a specifically military-oriented cultural theorist like Paul Virilio who has been massively influenced by the prolongation of the conflict. Virilio, in Bosworth's sense of history, continued, through his theorising of new cultural and military technological formations, to fight the Second World War over sixty years later. As we have seen, Virilio does not believe that the Second World War is even over legally, let alone 'culturally'.

Another query comes to mind for theorists who would extrapolate from Virilio and others the idea of a speeded-up or accelerated culture. If accelerated culture is the 'popular', the 'contemporary', the 'now', where everything is speeded up so much that reality is just a blur, how long are its historical roots? In his own historiography of speed, Virilio himself goes back several centuries, and others suggest that the roots of military and communications technological revolutions are at least traceable to the sixteenth century. Contemporary cultural writers hark back even earlier. The controversial young British playwright Mark Ravenhill, taking an even longer historical perspective than Virilio, has written that,

> Year on year, decade on decade, century on century, since the Renaissance, western culture has accelerated. There are always more narratives and more images than the year before, and new technologies are constantly discovered that allow them to be distributed to a wider constituency and at a greater speed ... But is this an ever-widening virtuous circle? Can it keep on expanding infinitely and still be making our lives richer and better? (*The Guardian*, 18 November 2000)

Certainly the moral, or ethical, question of whether accelerated culture produces the 'good life' or the 'great society' is one which interests Virilio too. But Ravenhill, like Virilio, knows that the best example of this accelerated culture is modern 'celebrity culture' or 'star culture', where Andy Warhol's 1960s pronouncement about 'fifteen minutes of fame' has rapidly become more like fifteen seconds in a twenty-first century where 'reality' is so doubled back on itself in acceleration that it is apparently more like the simulated universe implied by Jean Baudrillard's phrase 'hyperreality'. As we shall see later in this book, Paul Virilio is not a believer in the 'hyperreal' of Baudrillard's vision but he does examine frequently in his writings the world of supermodels and celebrity politicians mired in the 'new electronic Babel' where the 'goal is to speak as fast as possible' and where the effect is technological 'generalised violence of acceleration' where the screen has 'replaced the scaffold'.

Virilio has produced a whole series of books and articles where obscure aspects of speed, technology and modernity are pored over in hundreds of aphoristic, often apparently unconnected statements. More often, however, this general colloquial interest in speed among critics and commentators today tends to translate in public debate into a technical question about technology. Argument, for example, rages about whether 'things' in general rather than culture in particular have speeded up. Populist science authors like James Gleick have claimed that they have done so: as the title of one of his books has it, *Faster – The Acceleration of Just about Everything*. Other pundits claim the opposite. For instance, the social affairs writer Paul Barker has argued that 'the speeding up of everyday life is a fading illusion', and that although some public intellectuals have encouraged us to think of the twenty-first century as fast, in fact in the first decade of the twenty-first century, we are witnessing a 'slowdown' in comparison with the twentieth century. The twentieth century had a passion for speed in Barker's view which will be reversed in the 'slow-motion' twenty-first. Although electronic communication is frequently cited as the high point of speed, according to Barker, all is not what it seems, especially if British contemporary art (another favourite topic for Virilio) is the focus:

> Video art, so lavishly displayed at Tate Modern and at the Royal Academy's Apocalypse show, underlines the paradox of e-speed. A video is quickly shot: no more struggles with intransigent stone or oil paint. This is, presumably, a bonus to the artist. But the videos are then run in real time, or even in slow motion. Swift to make, they feel endless to see. The pioneer – the great anti-Futurist aficionado of slowness – was Andy Warhol. Come back, Marinetti, all is forgiven: the artist may gain, but the spectator gets the pain. (*The Independent on Sunday*, 1 October 2000)

Slow living, and indeed slow food (as opposed to fast food), movements are slowly taking hold in some parts of the world today and cultural theorists are rushing to interpret them and generalise their significance, as adherents of accelerated culture have done before them. The points made by Barker and his fellow critics would not actually be lost on Paul Virilio, however. Significantly,

Virilio has claimed in interview that his interest is in both 'negative' and 'positive' speed – 'deceleration' and 'acceleration'. 'What interests me is their totality', 'the two of them', Virilio has stated boldly and unequivocally. Hand in glove with this acceleration and deceleration come 'real speed and virtual speed', or for Virilio 'the rapidity of what happens unexpectedly, such as an urban crisis, or an accident'. Accelerated culture is where, in Virilio's terms, 'chronography' takes over from geography, where 'real time' supersedes 'real space' with all the attendant dangers of that process – what later in this book is labelled more generally as 'dangerous modernity.' It is where history 'is going to unfold within a one-time system: global time', according to Virilio. Or where 'time and distance melt away', as the Pet Shop Boys have sweetly sung it, with 'no digital delay'.

Accelerated culture, however, is underlined by instantaneity and ubiquity, not simply the process of speeding up or slowing down. 'Instantaneousness', according to Virilio, is a key element in the disappearance of 'history': 'History as the extensiveness of time – of time that lasts, is portioned out, organised, developed – is disappearing in favour of the instant, as if the end of history were the end of duration in favour of instantaneousness, and of course, of ubiquity' (Virilio 1997a: 52). The disappearance of history and the disappearance of territorialities means, in Virilio's view, that 'we're heading towards universality ... universe-city; the universal city'. To Virilio, what he calls 'critical space' has become 'ubiquitous because of the "acceleration of means of communication" that collapse the Atlantic (the Concorde), reduce France to a square of an hour and a half on each side (the airbus) or, yet again, tell us that the high-speed train (TGV) wins time over time'. Systems of telecommunication – as repetition of these contemporary French advertising publicity slogans by Virilio confirms – in the transmission of messages and images 'also eradicate duration or delay' in a speeded-up world. Virilio constantly refers in interview to 'teletopia' where 'telemarketing, tele-employment, fax-work ... e-mail transmissions at home, in apartments, or in cabled high rises' create a world that is 'telepresent', meaning 'to be here and elsewhere at the same time'. Virilio's idea of speed – which, as we have already seen, he acknowledges is relational, a relation between phenomena

– is really a subject to do with the notion of arrival, where what comes or arrives does so at such speed that, as Patrick Crogan (1990) has put it, 'the experience of departure and duration tend to disappear'. Virilio has indeed used the French phrase *ce qui arrive* for several different suggestive projects. Virilio, in fact, does acknowledge that 'live' coverage does in effect mean a slightly delayed arrival of a 'signal' or a 'message', but the general replacement of analogue with digital – if indeed it continues at its current pace – would reduce arrival time still further as the 'data which make up information undergo temporal compression'. As with scientist Albert Einstein's notion of the 'information bomb', which Virilio also takes up with great vigour in his later work, the idea that 'we are living in nothing less than the sphere of Einstein's relativity' has been central to Paul Virilio's conviction. The post-Newtonian world where the absolute character of the speed of light has displaced the previous absolutes of 'time' and 'space', thereby creating what he calls a 'third interval' (Virilio, 1993a), is a starting-point for Virilio. As Crogan has put it, 'the question of relation has become crucial in the era of modernity' and Virilio is well aware of this point in his efforts to create the science of 'dromology'. The search for integrated dromological features of modern society that Virilio has pursued may be a vain one, as we shall discover later in this book, but any consideration of accelerated modernity should take its main features into account.

Dromology

Paul Virilio's research and writing has consistently focused on the technologies of the war machine, and speed has been the fundamental focus in that work. Even though, as he has admitted, topology gave way to dromology from the late 1960s, there is really no reason to argue for critics and commentators being able to identify some kind of 'epistemological break' in Paul Virilio comparable to that of the 'early' Karl Marx in the 1840s . In Virilio's own considered reflection it was not his thinking that was radicalised, but the 'situation itself' in the late twentieth-century society of speed as it raced towards the millennium. It was what he once saw as the 'dromocracy' that eventually became 'radicalised beyond measure'. It is worth a bibliographical digression on Virilio's work on dromology and its implications to explicate this.

If 'bunker archaeology' and 'cryptic architecture' were the dominant self-developed descriptions of Virilio's work in the 1950s and 1960s, by the mid 1970s Paul Virilio was an emerging theorist of 'dromology'. Again this term was his original invention. His first book, which he had advertised in the pages of the magazine/journal *Architecture Principe* in the 1960s as a text which was going to be published imminently and would be called *Architecture Cryptique*, was not in fact published until 1975. This book was actually entitled *Bunker Archéologie*. The first edition appeared in France in 1975 and no book with the alternative title ever saw the light of day. Published by the Centre de Création Industrielle in Paris in 1975, the book eventually received the accolade of a second edition from another publisher, Les Editions du Demi-Cercle, with a new afterword, in 1991 when Virilio's reputation was much greater and 'dromologist' was the label more usually applied to him. The English translation, entitled *Bunker Archaeology*, was taken from this second edition, as we have already noted, and was produced by the American publishers Princeton Architectural Press in New Jersey in 1994, somewhat obscuring the slow historical process by which Virilio worked on bunker archaeology and cryptic architecture in the 1950s and 1960s. In this well-illustrated, long-awaited publication based on Virilio's research and photographs from the 1950s, he wrote explicitly about the emerging concerns of 'military space' and 'territory'. A year later in 1976 the first edition of *L'Insécurité du Territoire* was published in Paris by Stock, and Virilio was revealed to his French readers to be concentrating on the development of these twin ideas, to which he had by then added 'the suicidal state', 'deterritorialisation' and 'nomadism'. *L'Insécurité du Territoire* has never been published in English and only partial English translations in collections of Virilio's books and essays exist. Virilio later recalled in interview with Nicholas Zurbrugg that this early book was in truth really more about the 'littoral mentality' and that this 'littoral' condition was fundamental to his whole outlook. Virilio went on in the conversation to describe himself as a 'creature of the shore, of the frontier.' He asserted that his 'mentality is littoral' partly owing to the fact that his 'mother came from Brittany' and his 'father came from Genoa' and that he considered himself 'something of a Breton' having a 'nomadic, naval mentality'. Elsewhere Virilio has explicitly stated that he is a 'voyager'. Being Italian on his father's side, Virilio did not consider himself 'a nationalist': 'I'm French by language, though I don't feel attached to any country I'm … an exile', he has declared to all comers. In the interview with Zurbrugg, Virilio recognised the artistic impulse of voluntary exiles, such as William Burroughs and Samuel Beckett, crossing frontiers, describing them, and by implication himself, as 'voyagers, visionaries'.

'Dromology' – albeit with this added littoral mentality – fully took centre stage in Virilio's publishing career in 1977. In that year *Vitesse et Politique* was published. With the wonderful benefit of hindsight, this text can now be seen to be the base for launching Paul Virilio as a public intellectual of international reputation, as he is considered around the world today. The French manuscript was the first of Virilio's to be accepted for publication in what was virtually by then his own imprint, the 'Collection L'Espace Critique' series by Galilée in Paris. The book's analysis depended on a simple but pervasive 'big idea' in Virilio's writing that 'Speed is the Essence of War'. For Virilio, as we have noted already, modern society was, at least in the twentieth century, dominated 'by war' and 'hyper-violence'. *Vitesse et Politique* analysed the ways in which modern society closes spaces as the speed of the society accelerates, and it ranged far and wide over several centuries for its myriad examples of war or instances of speed.

Modern technology, and particularly military technology, was the book's key to the interpretation of this speeding-up. Virilio has acknowledged that *Vitesse et Politique* was in some ways the 'theoretical complement' to *L'Insécurité du Territoire* and that it was 'an important little book because it was the first to raise the question of speed', although he pointedly cites Jack Kerouac in literature, Marinetti and the Italian Futurists in art, and Marshall McLuhan in the academy as taking steps in that direction too.

In Virilio's own view *Vitesse et Politique* was 'not so important for what it says as for the question it raises'. This short 'essay on dromology' was a 'rapid book' according to its author. It was not translated into English until 1986, by which time Virilio's name was becoming more widely known internationally. Sylvère Lotringer (who along with Jim Fleming was co-founder of Semiotext(e)) had already by this time conducted his extensive and fascinating interviews with Virilio in Paris and New York between January and June 1982. These conversations were subsequently published in the Semiotext(e) Foreign Agent series in 1983 as *Pure War* (1983). *Speed and Politics* (Virilio 1986), the English translation of *Vitesse et Politique*, with the subtitle 'An Essay on Dromology', received its long-delayed publication in 1986 in the Semiotext(e) Foreign Agent series almost a decade after the text was initially read in French. The book was essentially the vehicle which brought Virilio's then groundbreaking theoretical stance to an English-speaking global audience, and it remains, in many cases, the only book in English by Virilio that humanities-oriented students and their teachers, or even casually interested general readers, have consulted. English-speaking readers in the mid 1980s had little of Paul Virilio's work available to them, but in *Speed and Politics* they would have found this enigmatic writer continuing the themes of military space and deterritorialisation which they might have identified in the *Pure War* interviews with Lotringer but with a more overarching schema that amounted almost to a general theory of what Virilio labelled a 'dromocratic society'. It was probably the last time any kind of general theory or grand narrative was promised by Virilio, whose work became ever more fragmented and aphoristic as the years went by. Tantalisingly, what the reader of *Speed and Politics*, even today, is left wondering is how this notion of the dromocratic society – if indeed there can be said to be such a new formation – fitted in with the rapidly changing political and cultural upheavals of the mid to late 1970s. As cultural and political theorists in general came to rely less on general theories of social formations, Virilio's idea of the dromocratic becomes less central in writings and discussions of him after *Speed and Politics*. No other theorists have taken up the question of the dromocratic society in any sustained fashion in the wake of Virilio's rapid effort. The same sense of a 'whole' to Virilio's theorising is never really reached again in his oeuvre after the completion of *Speed and Politics*, although Virilio has claimed that all of his books do 'form a whole' in that ideas in earlier books are echoed in subsequent ones.

Italian autonomism

Finishing *Speed and Politics* in the original French text in September 1977, Paul Virilio was to be found reflecting aloud on the major political events which had been taking place in Western Europe, such as the revolution in Portugal, Enrico Berlinguer's 'historic compromise' in Italy, and the general problems and possibilities of 'Eurocommunism' in Europe in the 1970s, as well as the rise of the Khmer Rouge in Cambodia and the future of Vietnam after the fall of Saigon. Reflections on Pol Pot and Cambodia, as well as the mushrooming of Middle East hijackings and shootings from 1969, even pervade the less overtly political parts of the interviews Virilio granted to Sylvère Lotringer of Semiotext(e) in the early 1980s, and it is clear that Paul Virilio was just as acute an observer of world politics in the 1970s as he became in the very different neo-liberal decades of the 1980s and 1990s.

We came across the Italian Autonomists earlier in this book when we excavated Virilio's part in the 'May '68' events and considered the question of his relationship to groups such as the Situationists (or Situationist International) and the Autonomists. In particular the 1970s was the period when the Italian Autonomists, including figures like the academic Toni (Antonio) Negri were attempting to come to terms with the political implications of the guerilla warfare and other activities of the Red Brigades in Italy in the late 1970s. In fact, Toni Negri, a publicly committed revolutionary and academic, was famously charged with leadership of the Red Brigades and the kidnapping and murder of Prime Minister Aldo Moro, and was given a long-term prison sentence. Aldo Moro, Christian Democrat politician and originator of the 'historic compromise' of the left and right, was brutally murdered in 1978, his body eventually turning up in a Renault car in Rome after the kidnap. Negri ultimately escaped to France in 1983 and taught in Paris, where he was supported in print by, among others, Gilles Deleuze, the co-writer of many books with Virilio's friend Félix Guattari. Nearly twenty years later Negri went back to Italy to serve part of the rest of his sentence as an inmate of Rebibbia Prison in Rome, and from that incarceration subsequently wrote an influential best-selling book, entitled *Empire*, with colleague

Michael Hardt. Virilio questioned the tactics of the Red Brigades at the time in the 1970s, but he has said in relation to the period that at the time he was working on dromology, especially around the publication of *Speed and Politics*, he felt that his own approach was a bit 'high-flying, trans-historical in some ways' and not conducive to political action, instead being more oriented to a vision of a 'scientific order'. As we have said earlier in this book, the Autonomists' ultra-leftist political actions were certainly of a completely different order to anything that Paul Virilio has become involved with at any time in his life, although his 'anti-statism' has consistently left him vulnerable to such anarchical political connections.

Some of the Italian Autonomists misused the writings of Paul Virilio in such a way as to emphasise a pro-technology position in their struggle with the Italian state in the 1970s. Their own struggle was formally distinct from that of the Red Brigades. These Italian 'Autonomia' ultra-leftists suffered from the repression engendered by the state as a result of the conflation of the Red Brigades and the Autonomists. Paul Virilio's interviewer, and Semiotext(e) joint publisher, Sylvère Lotringer, has admitted that it was 'the Italian Autonomists' who 'were the first ones to show' him Virilio's book *Speed and Politics*. Lotringer certainly knew them and published some of their texts in the USA. Semiotext(e), for instance, published Toni Negri's book *Marx Beyond Marx*, essentially his 'lessons on the Grundrisse', which were originally presented in the 1970s as lectures at the Ecole Normale Supérieure in Paris given at the invitation of the then-influential theorist and French Communist Party intellectual Louis Althusser. Further published by Semiotext(e) were Negri's collaborations with his supporter Deleuze's co-author Guattari, entitled *Communists Like Us*, and with Mario Tronti, a book called *The Social Factory*. There was also included in the Semiotext(e) list the definitive 'autonomia' collection, *Italy: Autonomia: Post-Political Politics*, a volume which included an essay by Paul Virilio called 'Popular Defense and Popular Assault'. Sylvère Lotringer was therefore well placed to discuss Virilio with the Italian Autonomists. Paul Virilio has recalled that it was indeed a surprise that there had been misreadings of his work, especially in the Italian context:

> In fact I had heard through the grapevine that in Italy they HAD
> interpreted my work as being pro-technology. I was very surprised
> at first. That's why I wrote POPULAR DEFENSE AND
> ECOLOGICAL STRUGGLES in which I questioned the tactics of the
> Red Brigades. I know they heard it. I've also published interviews
> ... to denounce that mistaken interpretation. (Virilio 1997a: 80)

Dromology was always, then, a political theory, not some kind of
'objective' commentary on technology and society. But Virilio did
not believe, and has never believed, in 'revolution'. He has,
however, admitted that his observation of the practice of the
Autonomists caused him to think more about 'resistance'. Undoubtedly, this political rethinking in the mid 1970s is the key to the
next book in the Virilio series, *Popular Defense and Ecological
Struggles* (Virilio 1990a), which was first published in French in
1978 in Paris, once again by Galilée in the 'Collection L'Espace
Critique' series, as *Défense Populaire et Luttes Ecologiques*, and later
in English translation by Semiotext(e) as a 'little black book' in
1990. This book in a sense completed the first (or, more accurately,
the 1970s) phase of Virilio's publishing history, although the
discourse on accelerated culture and accelerated history, and on
aspects of the 'dromocratic', never really ended. It simply became
more fragmented throughout Virilio's subsequent publications,
more and more of which tracked the acceleration of technology in
our daily lives.

Virilio has remained 'conscious of the positive aspects of
technology' while 'at the same time conscious of its negative
aspects'. The accelerated complexity of modernity has continued to
engage him throughout the whole of the 1980s and 1990s and into
the twenty-first century, especially with the concentration on the
accident and its emanation from speeded-up modernity. The
intertwining of what he has linked together in his unique analysis
of 'violence and speed' is, however, predicated on another, related
theoretical exploration: in Virilio's phrase the pursuit of 'the
aesthetics of disappearance'. If, as one critic has put it, Virilio is
'the only contemporary radical philosopher of speed', the
contemplation of the 'aesthetics of disappearance' is the necessary
offshoot of this enterprise.

The aesthetics of disappearance

In 1980 Editions Balland published Virilio's next book, *Esthétique de la Disparition*, in a pocket edition, later replicated by Editions Galilée in 1989. Semiotext(e) published the English translation as *The Aesthetics of Disappearance* (Virilio 1991a) in 1991, this time in a large-format book with a distinctive 'disappearing' design by Steve Jones rather than in the 'little black book series'. The effects of speed in culture were excavated by Virilio in this text with a focus on the human 'subject' as a 'picnoleptic' or the 'picnolept'. As we have already seen in this book, picnolepsy meant, in other more common words, a condition of someone approaching a mild state of sub-epilepsy or tiny death or even interruption of consciousness. The key for Virilio was that this was seen to be the condition of the human subject in speeded-up, dromocratic society and was not confined to an aberrant or deviant individual case history or pyschoanalysis. Some commentators on this concept have reached out for some kind of Virilian take on a 'postmodern' subjectivity, or even a pseudo post-structuralist subject position, but this is not Virilio's intention in the theoretical enterprise at all, and such interpretation only serves to confuse the place of picnolepsy in Virilio's thought. He is not really considering subject 'positions' as constructed by discourse or ideology, as structuralist or post-structuralist thought would do. In Virilio the picnolept concept recurs as a kind of suggestive reminder, or implicit idea, of how it feels to live in dromocratic society. The book itself looked at the illusion of movement in speed and introduced the idea of an 'aesthetic' of disappearance in war, film and politics, a triangle which was to become almost as pervasive in Virilio's work as violence and speed. According to Virilio, an 'aesthetics of disappearance', which itself followed an 'aesthetics of appearance', came into being originally as long ago as the nineteenth century along with the transportation revolution. Virilio's interest in this process evidently stemmed from the young Paul Virilio's career as a painter of stained glass:

> The aesthetics of appearance concerns both sculpture and painting. Forms emerge from their material – marble for a Michelangelo sculpture, canvas for a Leonardo da Vinci painting – and the

persistence of the support is the essence of the advent of the image, the very image that emerges by way of the sketch and that is fixed with a varnish, just as marble is polished ... an aesthetics of disappearance was born. Through the invention of the instant photo that made the cinematographic photogram possible, the aesthetics was set in motion. Things exist even more so because they disappear. Film is an aesthetics of disappearance staged by sequences. It is no longer a question of transportation, it is the speed of the snapshot, then the speed of twenty-four images per second of film that will revolutionise perception and completely change the aesthetics. Confronted with the aesthetics of disappearance, all that remains is retinal persistence. Retinal persistence is necessary to see the images of the sequence, or the photogram, come to life. So we move from the persistence of a material – marble or the painter's canvas – to the cognitive persistence of vision. It is the possibility to take snapshots, in other words to accelerate the shooting process, which favoured the appearance of an aesthetics of disappearance that continues today in television and video. (Virilio 1999: 22–3)

This perceptual 'vision thing', and the speeding-up of the process, was to be a pervasive theme in Virilio's subsequent work in the 1980s. After *The Aesthetics of Disappearance* project was finished, Virilio began to work on what was an originally 'an essay on war and cinema'. Soon afterwards, in 1984, he published *Guerre et Cinéma 1*, subtitled 'Logistique de la Perception', in Editions Cahiers du Cinéma, with a stunning, plain white cover framing a photograph of 'Le Congrès Nazi du Nuremberg au Zeppelin-Field' in 1938. In 1989 Verso books in London, England, published the English translation as *War and Cinema: The Logistics of Perception* (Virilio 1989b) with a different cover showing a photograph of an airman in a Lancaster bomber from 1943 which had been included in a series of inside illustrations to the book in the original French edition. The book gave a detailed technical history of weaponry, cinematography and photography and the links – as Virilio perceived them – between film, photography and military campaigns. It is now one of Virilio's best-known and most-cited volumes. For Virilio the subject of 'war and cinema' is absolutely indispensable. In Virilio's view, 'war became a war film' after 1914 as what he has labelled the 'logistics of perception' became revolutionised:

World War I was a revolution in perception, and much earlier than Dziga Vertov ... After 1914, war became a war film; there were no longer paintings of battles or maps highlighted in red or blue, but a film. Documentary filmmaking developed mainly in England during World War II, partly thanks to Vertov. Yet one cannot understand Vertov and 'The Man with the Camera' or the documentary filmmaking that originated at that time without going back to the 1914 war. (Virilio 1999: 27)

Virilio had always had a notion of the battlefield as a 'field of perception' in any case. 'War', for him, had necessarily revealed 'with immediacy that every battle and every conflict is a field of perception'. Both the First World War and the Second World War were examples for him and indeed they were watersheds on the way to a military process leaving maps and geography as things of the past, demanding a move in thinking for Virilio from topology to dromology. As Virilio saw it,

The battlefield is first a field of perception. Seeing them coming and knowing that they are going to attack are determining elements of survival. In war, you can't be surprised, for surprise is death. The 1914 war and World War II radically modified the field of perception. Before World War I war was always waged with maps. Yves Lacoste said 'Geography is meant to wage war'. It happens that maps are drawn using topographical landmarks or surveys to direct artillery firing. If the 1914 war was not a total war, then at least it had totalitarian tendencies, and it destroyed all the topographical landmarks of eastern France. Thus, after every artillery battle, it was absolutely imperative to make photo-mosaics in order to get re-oriented and not massacre each other needlessly. The first planes were used not to fight but to observe from above, as the first balloons were used to photograph the enemy lines. So the cinema, the photo-cinema, the photo-mosaic and the documentary were all used to wage war and favoured an expanded vision of the battlefield. In the past, in order to see the enemy, you had to climb a high point or watchtower and then you could see them coming. Later the plane and camera were used to try and locate the enemy. (Virilio 1999: 26)

Meanwhile, Virilio's project on the 'logistics of perception' and 'aesthetics of disappearance' was pushing ahead. In 1984, the same year as *Guerre et Cinéma* was published, Christian Bourgeois published the related volume *L'Espace Critique*, echoing in its title the Galilée series in Paris edited by Virilio. When it came to the English translation and publication by Semiotext(e) in 1991, it was again in large format and with a distinctly odd-looking 'fishy' cover design by Sue Anne Harkey, but the title was strangely *The Lost Dimension* (Virilio 1991b), not *Critical Space* as might have been expected (although the last essay in the volume was indeed entitled 'Critical Space'). Moreover, 'critical space' had become by this time an important concept for Virilio in the development of his dromological analyses and it reappears in his work on international military conflicts in the 1990s. This was further contextualised by his emerging idea of 'negative horizons'. In the same year as *L'Espace Critique* was published in France, Galilée released *L'Horizon Négatif: Essai de Dromoscopie*. The essay was subsequently translated into English under the title 'Negative Horizons' (Virilio 1987) and included in the Semiotext(e) volume *Semiotext(e): USA* which came out in 1987. By this time other significant Virilio material was also in the public domain, such as the English translation of the *Pure War* interviews conducted with Sylvère Lotringer, a book which explained much of the background thinking to the idea of the 'aesthetics of disappearance' and 'critical space', and much else in Virilio's theoretical meanderings besides. Another phase in Virilio's publishing history had been completed by the mid 1980s, including *La Crise des Dimensions*, papers from the Ecole Spéciale d'Architecture which were made available in France in 1983.

The last art

Not only the culture of speed but Virilio's own writing and publishing history was accelerating by this time in his career. By the late 1980s and early 1990s Paul Virilio's work had shifted into another gear while still maintaining the same basic foci: speed and culture, war, technology and perception. In 1988 *La Machine de Vision* was published in the 'Collection L'Espace Critique' by Galilée, and an English translation was put out by the British Film Institute in London some years later in 1994, entitled *The Vision Machine* (Virilio 1994a). In 1990 *L'Inertia Polaire* was published by

Christian Bourgeois in Paris, and a decade later in 2000, Sage published an English translation with the title *Polar Inertia* (2000d). It was clear for English readers that Virilio had in fact been arguing for a long time that speeded-up technological society had made 'inertia' the overriding modern condition. An instantaneousness in the present had replaced space and territory and the book finds Virilio once again trumpeting the notion that in accelerated modernity things happen so fast that there is no need to go anywhere.

In 1991, at the time of the Gulf War, a new Virilio book was produced, bringing together several essays and interviews from 1990 and 1991. Chronicling the military strategy and desert conflict involving the USA and its allies attacking Iraq after it had invaded Kuwait in 1990, the book was entitled *L'Ecran du Désert: Chroniques de Guerre*. It was produced as a book reasonably quickly and published in Paris by Galilée in the 'Collection L'Espace Critique'. The English translation took eleven years to emerge, with the title *Desert Screen* (Virilio 2002c), and included a postscript interview with James Der Derian. Instead of the ordinary French subtitle, the English subtitle was 'War at the Speed of Light', a much more apposite label and a phrase which by the second Gulf War in 2003 had passed imperceptibly into media discourse: journalists referred in the reporting of the American advance to Baghdad to war conducted at the speed of light. Unlike Jean Baudrillard's controversial musings on the 1991 conflict following Saddam Hussein's Iraqi army invasion of Kuwait, Virilio did not claim that the Gulf War 'did not take place'. Indeed, Virilio's book is much more conventional in many senses than Baudrillard's, part of a more widespread theoretical and political difference between the two men that we shall explore in detail later in this book. In Virilio's perceptive and careful look at the 1991 Gulf War, which before the full English translation was published was selectively translated in James Der Derian's *Virilio Reader* (Der Derian 1998) and elsewhere by Sean Cubitt, there was a conceptualisation of the 'Desert Screen' (in French *L'Ecran du Désert*) to follow the military's own 'Desert Shield' and 'Desert Storm' in the Gulf War itself. Here, speed, having been seen previously by Virilio to be the 'essence of war', now really *was* war by the early 1990s. The first Gulf War was a

14

watershed for Virilio. In what he called a 'total electronic war', all information converged on, and radiated from, the 'screen', the 'pole of inertia'. All the history of the acceleration and refinement of observational technology, and the 'logistics of perception' which Virilio had drawn upon prior to the early 1990s, had come to fruition in this transformative 'event' of new technological and media warfare. Omnipresence and instantaneity were displayed in the communications technologies of the media where information reached journalists and 'consumers' watching the screens simultaneously. Virilio could claim to have been right all along since the 1970s about the acceleration that had produced the 'oh-so smart' weapons as he has sarcastically called them. Tomahawk cruise missiles flew hundreds of miles to their 'targets', for instance, and were on display on CNN (the war channel!) 'live' every night in the Gulf War: what the British singer Billy Bragg labelled with heavy irony 'the Third World War live on CNN'. However, significant as the Gulf War 'live' was to Virilio, it was what he was to describe later as 'infowar' that really engaged him in the early 1990s. As he admitted to Louise Wilson (1994) in interview a few years after the end of the Gulf War itself, it was 'live' broadcasting which created the 'virtual' Gulf War:

> The high level of the technologies used during the Gulf War makes this conflict quite unique, but the very process of de-realisation of the war started in 1945. War occurred in Kuwait, but it also occurred on the screens of the entire world. The site of defeat or victory was not the ground but the screen. (Wilson 1994)

This was the important argument in his chronicles of war about 'Desert Screen'. As Virilio noted in the interview with Wilson, the 'live' nature of the conflict marked it as a watershed of crucial importance for the future, and the future of war:

> The Gulf War was the first 'live' war. World War II was a world war in space. It spread from Europe to Japan, to the Soviet Union etc. World War II was quite different from World War One which was geographically limited to Europe. But in the case of the Gulf War, we are dealing with a war which is extremely local in space, but global in time, since it is the first 'live' war. And to those, like my friend Baudrillard, who say that this war did not actually occur,

I reply: this war may not have occurred in the actual global space, but it did occur in global time. And this thanks to CNN and the Pentagon. This is a new form of war, and all future wars, all future accidents will be live wars and live accidents. (Wilson 1994)

For the remainder of the decade following the Gulf War, Virilio continued to be extremely productive. In 1993 the 'Collection L'Espace Critique' published a second edition of Virilio's mid 1970s text *L'Insécurité du Territoire* with an afterword by Virilio himself. It still received no English publication, and has never been published in full in English. Also in 1993 *L'Art du Moteur* was published by Galilée in the 'Collection L'Espace Critique' and an English translation was put out in 1995 by the University of Minnesota Press under the title *The Art of the Motor* (Virilio 1995a). In 1995, too, *La Vitesse de Libération* was published in 'Collection L'Espace Critique' and an English translation followed, published by Verso in 1997. The French title literally means 'liberation speed' but Virilio's preferred English title would have been *Escape Velocity*. In the event it was called *Open Sky* (Virilio 1997b). In this early to mid 1990s phase of Virilio's publishing, there is a kind of 'reintroduction' of 'speed', but the focus is often on what Virilio acknowledges is 'the last art', the 'end of art'. The 'last art' is not conceived in Jean Baudrillard's fatalistic notion of the 'last' but more in the sense that 'technology has become the last art and that includes perception'. In Virilio's view, 'from now on, art goes via the engine'.

Indeed, Paul Virilio at this particular juncture in speeded-up military technology and associated accelerated communications became fascinated with the idea of 'a machine that sees for itself', exemplified by the unpiloted planes or drones used in the Gulf War in 1991, and, as if to prove Virilio right, the Afghanistan 'war on terror' in 2001 and the second Gulf War in 2003. The first Gulf War saw extensive use of cruise missiles too, often fired from ships in oceans many miles away, a definite sign of the end of 'industrial war' or the speeding-up of war, and moreover the 'robot war' Virilio believed was shortly to come:

The sign of war to come is that the Gulf War was waged from the skies by satellites, that orbiting deus ex machina that manages the time of war. It was not only the first miniature world war, but also the first war in real time. I see two events: the beginning of the war and the end of the war. First the cruise missiles were launched from the battleship Missouri, and then the Iraqi soldiers surrendered. Cruise missiles are highly sophisticated robots for which the 'vision machine' (the title of one of my books) will soon be invented. Equipped with an electronic map, they were supposed to follow a secret path and hit the target by entering through one window instead of another. Such accuracy required both permanent radar plotting to check if the missile was aligned with its electronic map, and an automatic vision machine to pick the window when the missile got in close range, in case the map was inadequate. The launching of these cruise missiles marks the beginning of robot war. (Virilio 1999: 99–100)

The mass use of cruise missiles in the first Gulf War in 1991 thus saw the beginning of a new phase of the 'vision machine' in war: Virilio's imaginary, but 'oh-so-present' robot wars. For Virilio 'the fact of sending out robots against men is clearly an event signalling the electronic warfare of tomorrow: cyberwar'. However, in Virilio's eyes, this futuristic military scenario of the vision machine had already been developing for some time, even as far back as the 1960s:

all this had already been tested in Vietnam with the drones. Drones are unpiloted planes that scope out enemy territory. They are launched with captors, radar, video, thermography ... and keep watch on the battlefield of the enemy. For the duration of the war in Lebanon, there were scouts (this is the name given to the drones sent by Israel) measuring six feet that flew over Beirut to try to attack Arafat. They were equipped with videography and thermography enabling them to detect the heat of Arafat's car in order to constantly identify his location. At the end of the Gulf War, forty Iraqi soldiers isolated in the desert saw a drone arrive that was circling around them. They left their trenches and surrendered to the drone. This is the very image of the end of the warrior. Surrendering to a flying camera is a terrifying image. Seeing this drone arrive, the Iraqi soldiers dropped their weapons because they knew the highly sophisticated artillery of the Americans would blow them up. With the eye flying over them, they had no choice but to surrender to this eye ... From now on the eye of God is everywhere. This is telesurveillance – not of the city, but of the battlefield. (Virilio 1999: 100)

By the time of the second Gulf War in 2003, which itself followed hard on the heels of the English publication of *Desert Screen: War at the Speed of Light*, Paul Virilio had become required reading for students, enrolled at university or not, of modern 'war studies'.

CHAPTER THREE
Dangerous modernity

What we have labelled in this book as accelerated modernity, or the accelerated culture implied by the proclamations of Paul Virilio and others, might be thought to be manifestly dangerous. The excessive technologising of war, and its civilian effects, certainly contains elements of danger for both citizens and the military. That does not mean, however, that society is inexorably more dangerous in the twenty-first century as compared to the twentieth. Unmanned 'vision machines' such as drones and cruise missiles may lessen the casualties of war, at least on one side, as was proven in both the first and second Gulf wars and the Balkan and Afghanistan campaigns, even though thousands still died on the 'other' side. We shall nevertheless introduce the idea of dangerous modernity in this chapter to help us to interrogate Virilio's theory of the accident, his most explicit theorisation of the disaster inherent in modernity. By looking at a specific case study of the attacks on the World Trade Center on 11 September 2001 and its 'live' broadcasting all over the globe – an event Virilio himself explicitly cites as an historic example of his theory of the invention of the accident – we can assess the consequences of the application of the concept of accelerated modernity.

Dangerous modernity as a concept or theme is introduced at this point in the book in order to situate Virilio's theorising of the accident in relation to the rest of his œuvre as a whole. In partial answer to the question of how the notion of the accident fits in, Virilio, in the course of thinking through the long trajectory of the post-Second World War period, has in his writings since the 1970s shown us the crucial dimensions of aspects of accelerated modernity: what he calls the 'ecology of the image' and the global media 'event'. These notions can be given concrete illustration and Virilio himself has cited many of these instances in his writings and in his museum curation. The examples include many which he has labelled 'terrorist' or 'state terrorist', namely: the Gulf War in 1991, the World Trade Center bomb in 1993, the Kenya and Tanzania US embassy bombs, the Oklahoma City bombing, the Aum Shinrikyo gas attack in the Japanese subway, the Clinton/US attack on Iraq, the same Democratic administration's assault on Osama bin Laden training camps in Afghanistan and his supposed chemical weapons factory in Sudan in 1998, and the NATO bombing of the former

Yugoslavia under Milosevic. The hijacked commercial airliners' suicide assault on the World Trade Center on 11 September 2001 is the event we have chosen to illustrate Paul Virilio's notion of the accident in this chapter. It is highly appropriate to select this event above all others as Virilio himself wrote about the World Trade Center bombing in 1993, making predictions which were uncannily manifested in the later 2001 attack. Other examples of the media event as accident frequently cited by Virilio involve the Chernobyl disaster and the speeding-up of financial markets which have huge economic dangers and consequences. Hence he refers in his writings and interviews to the 1987 stock exchange crash and the 1997 Asian markets disaster ten years later. In the latter event Virilio has noted that with half a million screens throughout the globe tracking a totally computerised stock market, the 'accident' was watched everywhere 'live' as it happened. The 'virtual bubble' of the financial markets in Virilio's vision of the future will increasingly give way to the 'visual bubble' where everyone watches the accident (whatever its nature) on their screens either via the internet or on television. On 11 September 2001 this is exactly what happened and it was the first heralding of Virilio's predicted 'accident of accidents' of the twenty-first century.

The World Trade Center attack is an example of an 'event' in Paul Virilio's terminology. Virilio's definition of an event is less in space than time. The attack on 11 September 2001 illustrates many of the ideas generated in Virilio's books about the accelerated global media with 'live' coverage of the event in a world where 'long term', says Virilio, constitutes a week. This is a world where, for Virilio, 'nothing follows on from anything else anymore and yet where nothing ever ends, the lack of duration of the perpetual present circumscribing the cycle of history and its repetitions'. However, it is interesting to take 11 September 2001 as a case study for its international political resonances, too. Virilio, especially in his later writings as we shall see, is fond of intervening in global political debates as a more conventional public intellectual with left-liberal humanist leanings. In Virilio's writings on earlier attacks and atrocities, and on the changes inaugurated by the collapse of the Berlin Wall in the late 1980s and the first Gulf War in the early 1990s, he has shown that he is well aware of what he sees as the 'frightening escalation' in the actions of the 'enemies of Western policies' who are 'putting the adversary to the test' as a result of the 'uncertainties of American foreign policy' in the post-Cold War age. The nuclear suitcase bomb, or similar threat, for instance, which preoccupied the neo-conservatives in the US government administration in the wake of 11 September 2001, which could be the result of 'fissile material being moved around God knows where', is certainly anticipated in many of Virilio's later writings in the 1990s and the twenty-first century.

It's not the end of the world

For Virilio, what all this means is that the age of nuclear deterrence is well and truly over. Deterrence, if nothing else, in Virilio's eyes, stabilised the world's main opponents and potential protagonists. The lonely, fatal last instance never actually came because each side or power bloc could predict the other's reactions. Regulation of nuclear arms is no longer possible in a world where restraint has gone and sovereign governments can talk openly of targeting certain hostile regimes, such as the so-called 'axis of evil', some with their own nuclear weapons, in the wake of the '11 September' attacks. For Virilio, the former age of nuclear deterrence:

> was a game, a military game. Whereas now the (game) doesn't exist anymore. It now goes from small-scale terrorism, like Black September which blows up aircraft, and to larger scale terrorism, like the World Trade Center and Oklahoma City bombings, and the Aum Shinrikyo gassing in Japan, for example – gas in the subway is a form of civilian terrorism. And so too is the hostage-taking of 700 people at the Japanese embassy in Lima, except that this is taking it to another stage. I'm tempted to say that what we can expect now is the hijacking of an entire town, and that is the classic scenario of nuclear terrorism, and of nuclear proliferation. (Virilio 1997a: 169)

We have introduced in this chapter another explanatory concept, that of 'dangerous modernity' in order to better describe these, and other, consequences of accelerated modernity. Virilio himself uses terms like accident and disaster but he is aware of danger in modernity. With dangerousness has come fear. Virilio has known this condition most of his life:

the years 1945–1950 were the years of nuclear deterrence, of the great anxiety which lasted for forty years. I lived that and I have to say that at the time, fear became a mass phenomenon. During the war, there were mass fears concerning the exterminated populations, but they did not last very long – often just the time of a bombing or the seizing of hostages. After 1945–50 the world was afraid of the end of the world. It was the time of nuclear deterrence and halting cinema, the cinema of suspense that was the cinema of anxiety, which is to say of survival. We lived because we were still surviving. We entered another world that was no longer that of the speed of trans- portation and the speed of communications – with the development of television and the airlines – but that of the atomic age, that is to say the possibility of an end of the world decided by man by way of total war between the East and the West. (Virilio 1999: 30–1)

But the end of the world, as Virilio knows, did not occur. He saw, however, a world in which what we have called here accelerated modernity continued apace over the last years of the century and in Virilio's view a new dangerousness, pregnant with disaster and accident (sometimes indistinguishable from attack) will ensue.

What political implications were there, then, for Virilio in the post-Cold War world? A new politics – or to quote sceptically, as Virilio does, British Prime Minister Tony Blair's adviser, Geoff Mulgan, 'a life after politics' – was demanded by many politicians and media pundits in the wake of the end of deterrence and the collapse of the Soviet bloc. Virilio has noted that what emerged was a supposedly 'democratic capitalism' which, 'with its universal network, should very soon escape the existing institutions and in short bring about the disappearance of all intermediate bodies, be they economic, political, judicial or cultural'. But Virilio has never wanted any truck with this 'end of history' as it has been conceived by what he sees as the forces of the right (best represented for him by someone like Francis Fukuyama), or indeed with 'trans-politics' as it has been conceived by the ultra-left (with whom he situates his friend Jean Baudrillard). Life after history or politics only solidifies military power ad infinitum for him:

the military IS nuclear power. There is no civilian nuclear power. It's obvious. For many 'trans-politics' was a vision à la Baudrillard – moreover that's how he understands it: a relatively positive vision.

For me it's totally negative. It's the contamination of traditional political thought by military thought period! There is nothing positive in my use of the term trans-politics. It's not post-politics, it's not the end of politics, it is its contamination. It's completely negative. Trans-politics means no more politics at all. (Virilio 1997a: 139)

What Virilio's political position actually is in this context is frequently difficult to fathom since he tends to go with the flow of events, and we shall further pursue the dilemma later in this book. But looking at what he has written, and declaimed in interview, his political position is more often a midway centrist line in between these two poles (ultra-left and neo-conservative), a kind of Francophile third way. Indeed, for Virilio, the accelerated replacement of urbanisation by broadcasting in the 'city of the instant' can be understood, he has argued, without succumbing simply to a pessimistic 'end of politics' which he attributes to the likes of Jean Baudrillard. Today, for Virilio, the time of worldwide broadcasting or 'real-time' means that concentration in the space of a city or a stadium 'corresponds to a concentration in broadcasting time'. In other words, in Virilio's vision, broadcasting replaces urbanisation and creates 'a city of the instant' where a billion people are gathered. It is a world of 'ubiquity and instantaneousness'. It is also characterised by what we have conceptualised here as accelerated and dangerous modernity. The resurrection of politics in dangerous modernity involves all sorts of conditions of existence but Virilio's writing has helped to give the lie to Francis Fukuyama's premature, and widely taken to be false, prediction of the global triumph of 'liberal democracy' in his pseudo-Hegelian treatise on the 'end of history and the last man'. For Virilio:

> After the end of history, prematurely announced a few years ago by Francis Fukuyama, what is being revealed here are the beginnings of the 'end of the space' of a small planet held in suspension in the electronic ether of our modern means of communication. (Virilio 2000c: 7)

Virilio has noted too that continuing his work of ten years earlier on 'the end of history', Fukuyama, far from admitting the absurdity of his theory, is now in the twenty-first century prophesying the 'end of humanity'. Virilio has often been scathing of Fukuyama's 'post-human history' and the post-human condition dominated by genetic and technological interventions into, and experiments on, the human body in what he thinks of as a third 'speed' revolution. This genetic revolution is coming for Virilio *after* the transport revolution of the nineteenth century and the communications revolution of the twentieth century. Moreover, Virilio has demonstrated an acute and long-standing awareness of what we have called in this context the dangerous modernity of the post-twentieth century. This society of the near future is not necessarily going to be a more violent society, for after all Virilio believes the twentieth century was the 'hundred years war' of 'hyperviolence'. But, equally for Virilio, it most certainly is a society of the 'accident' with massive and unpredictable consequences for global citizens. In Virilio's view, as he told Nicholas Zurbrugg in interview, the leaving of the twentieth century is not:

> the end of THE world – I believe in the end of A world. And from a certain perspective, the problem of pessimism or optimism with regard to the twentieth century seems to me to be a false debate. I am quite convinced that in subsequent centuries there will certainly be less violent epochs. Without a doubt! I am in no way despondent before either the twenty-first or twenty-second centuries. (1996a: 113)

The notion of dangerous modernity which we have raised here to situate more specifically Virilio's idea of the accident and the technological and social consequences of modernity is at first sight akin to some of the theoretical developments in social theory more generally. But first perceptions can be misleading, as Virilio knows. Some contemporary cultural theorists, for instance, have debated what they see as 'risk society'. The 'risk society' theorists (such as Ulrich Beck) are not, however, necessarily supported, or for that matter critiqued, in this archaeology of the future presented by Virilio. He is not comparable as a social theorist to someone like Ulrich Beck although where he features in the global academy is often in these terms. Social theory, as we shall see later in this book, is not at all Virilio's enterprise or intended outcome. Furthermore, Virilio has said that he is emphatically 'not apocalyptic', nor merely 'anti-technology'. The simple dichotomies really will not do any more for 'prophets' like Virilio when what we have described here as dangerous modernity is on the agenda. For Virilio in rather nostalgic, even paranoiac, mode,

> the new technologies are responsible for the loss of both the body proper in favour of the spectral body, and the world proper in favour of a virtual world. The main question is to regain contact … Since the world is a limited space, there comes a day when the losses become intolerable and there are no more benefits. The twenty-first century will probably be the century of this discovery: the losses will outnumber the benefits. We will have to compensate for the loss of the world proper and the loss of the body proper, since by that time, the situation will have become intolerable for everyone. (Virilio 1999: 48)

Virilio has certainly provoked more circumspect commentators by his last-stand liberal-humanistic outbursts which stress the importance of regaining 'contact' in a plan to save the world from 'loss'. For example, Virilio has suggested that 'if there is a solution possible today, it lies in the possibility of reorganising communal life'. Also he has claimed rather wistfully that the 'rediscovery of touch, contact through walking and mountain and climbing and navigation' are other means of getting back our 'relation to the body'. This relation of citizens 'to physical corporeality' is in Virilio's humanistic view drastically threatened by the shrinking of the world and the feeling of incarceration. These emotions are apparently felt by everyone except 'the young', according to Virilio. He explicitly laments the fact that 'we no longer talk to one another'. He has been accused of nostalgia for a previous age when there was not the same general air of 'loss', and of believing in an 'illusory' future in which restoration of what is lost can be achieved, and he has even been criticised as a 'prophet of doom' or 'apocalyptic'. Virilio, not surprisingly, has rejected such criticisms and defended his position robustly:

> People might find my approach too negative, but that is not true at all. It's just that I have to do this work on negativity all by myself, whereas most intellectuals have already become collaborators or even advertisers of the technological boom. Some of them even talk about 'civilisation' through the information technologies. With my work, I am trying to set the record straight. I am not afraid of being a

prophet of doom, since there's no one else to do it. (Virilio 1999: 52)

The importance of 'negativity' for Virilio is that he feels he has to show 'the hidden side of this technology, its negativity'. The accident, in Virilio's view, is something that we can say is almost pre-programmed by every technology, always already within it. When hundreds of people, for example, are airborne on a plane, in his argument, they are an accident waiting to happen. Certainly, speeding up technological change in modernity makes for a very dangerous modernity if we are to take some of Virilio's predictions of accident, catastophe and disaster, as well his overt warnings, seriously. This is partly because of the speeding-up of history and, in Virilio's own words, 'the truth of history'. In Virilio's mind,

> The history of my generation has just hit the insurmountable barrier of real time. We broke the two preceding barriers, the sound barrier and the heat barrier – the sound barrier with the supersonic plane and the heat barrier with the stratospheric rocket that makes liberation speed (28,000 km/h) possible and thus allows an individual to be put into orbit. Now history, our history, has just crashed into the barrier of real time. Everything that I've said in my books about the relationship between politics and speed has reached a limit. From now on, we will not accelerate anymore. From now on, history will have reached its limit speed ... I do know that this general accident, or the crashing into the time barrier, is an event that will force us to slow down, to regress, or to back up. This regression is a reaction to the attainment of the limit speed. It is still too early to say what form it will take. (Virilio 1999: 51–2)

In the main, I think we can say, using the concepts we have created to situate his work, that for Virilio accelerated modernity leads to dangerous modernity but by no means is this a 'things can only get worse' scenario. However, things, in Virilio's vision, will not necessarily get better either. He has become a self-styled 'periscope of probable catastrophes'.

Landscape of events

The acceleration of events in contemporary life, as we have seen already in this book, is the stuff of Paul Virilio's work. But we would do well to remember that it is the media coverage of those events which remains crucial for his scenarios. Virilio's focus has always necessarily included what he has called 'the communications revolution'. Perhaps the most important aspect of this particular transformation in contemporary society and culture is what has been described as the absolute power of the instant. This gives rise to a quite different notion of the 'end of history' to that of the much better-known idea of Virilio's bête noire Francis Fukuyama. Virilio has claimed not to be 'like Fukuyama' and not to be 'evoking the end of geography or the end of history', although there are definitely sufficient places in his work where the former seems to be quite unequivocally his aim. 'Loss', he has said, does not mean the same as 'the end' and the 'loss of history means that the immediacy of the present prevails over the past and the future'. In Virilio's oft-quoted statement:

> History as the extensiveness of time – of time that lasts, is portioned out, organised, developed – is disappearing in favour of the instant, as if the end of history were the end of duration in favour of instantaneousness, and of course, of ubiquity. (Virilio 1997a: 54)

This apparently enigmatic statement is actually a particularly clear summary of what Virilio has, uniquely, staked as his master claim. He said in answer to Sylvère Lotringer in 1997:

> So in a sense, the limit has been reached, and Fukuyama is entirely wrong: it's not the end of history, but the end of a regime of historical temporality. All of history was inscribed in local time, in local space and time. Time in China is not the same as time in Europe, just as time in Paris is not time in Aix-en-Provence, and so on. Now the history that is beginning is synchronised to world time, in other words, it's happening 'live'. What prevails is not the local time of time zones, or the passage from night into day, but the time as Hamlet, quoted by Deleuze, defined it: 'Time out of joint'. That's world time right there. Reaching the speed of light and using it to take a leak, now that's a major event. (Virilio 1997a: 185)

The acceleration of the reality of time studied by Virilio, or more accurately still the instantaneity and ubiquity of time, has been brought into the modern world by the 'communications revolution' of the hyper-violent twentieth century, and this, like the transport revolution of the previous century, has a mainly military gestation in Virilio's historical overview. 'PR wars' are thus always critical for Virilio and can be seen daily in a culture which has created 'celebrity' on a global scale as never before, even unimagined in the 1950s when Virilio was spending his time photographing German bunkers in France. The media 'explosion' has meant that there is much less time for celebrities to be famous and simultaneously there is a demand for more celebrities to be famous for less time. Politicians and presidents are only relevant in so far as they fit into this media machine. As we have already noted, in this era Virilio sees that the 'screen has replaced the scaffold', replacing the site where 'politics was killed in the past'. The media therefore is at the forefront of the major transformations in society which Virilio has exposed through a dogged, even painstaking analysis, of what he has frequently called 'atypical events'. The common denominator of these transformations is that 'space has become temporal' and the technology of media culture is central to this process. The 'landscape of events' which Virilio has recorded, however, is increasingly a landscape of 'accidents'. In Virilio's history of 'events', at the end of the twentieth century and the beginning of the twenty-first, such accidents almost imperceptibly changed from those which were 'specific, local and situated in time and space' to a dangerous modernity where the possibility of an accident (such as a stock-market crash like that of 1987, an event which Virilio himself has often selected as a prime example) is 'no longer particular but general'. Thus, for Virilio, there is the possibility of 'an accident brewing that would occur everywhere at the same time'. This is an 'original phenomenon' in Virilio's language. The times of the 'accident of accidents' is upon us if we are to believe the new Nostradamus.

Cultural theorists Mike Featherstone and Scott Lash (Featherstone and Lash 1999) have noted correctly that Virilio's notion of the 'collective world city' depends on the 'synchronisation of world time made possible through globalisation of information technology'. The internet is one example, but not necessarily the only or the best example, of technologies which give rise to the 'global accident'. Virilio, although only an occasional internet user himself, refers to 'virtual communities' organised in networks comprising many millions of people all over the world. He sees them as 'communities of believers' tele-present 'one to another thanks to the instantaneity' of the internet. Seemingly oblivious to the fact that the internet use is in fact dominated by citizens of the industrialised world (less than a fifth of the population of the planet), Virilio has concentrated on the 'dark side' of its technological substance and proclaimed that 'the internet has its own negativity' in the sense that all technologies contain within them the seeds of their accidents. He has also referred to the internet as a sign of 'the delirium of information' in our world. 'The information superhighway', he has argued, is going to 'set up an interactive system that is as daunting to society as the bomb is to matter'. In Virilio's vision the information, or logic, bomb, is in our midst. 'Logic bombs' have often been exploded by Virilio personally online. Ironically, seeing as he is only an 'occasional internet user', Paul Virilio the writer has been the subject of a special issue of the 'e-zine' (appropriately for Virilio) entitled *Speed*, and another online journal *Ctheory*, organised by Montreal's extravagantly performative cultural theory duo Arthur and Marilouise Kroker, has also published his work. There are Virilio sites on the internet and researchers regularly hit the virtual Paul Virilio. In daily life, Virilio has said that as far as the information superhighway is concerned he would rather keep his distance and participate laterally since 'frontal encounters are encounters where you never fail to be had'. Nevertheless, the trappings of a theorist in, and for, accelerated culture persist. 'Cybermonde', for instance, is a term that has become pervasive in Virilio's French language discourse since the early 1990s as well as 'cyberwar', and 'infowar', and he has been brazenly described in interview as a 'cyber-resistance fighter'.

Infowar

So what academic writers like Steve Jones have called 'cyber-society' is often actually the focus for Virilio's unfocused, ahistorical futuristic predictions. This society of the global accident, according to Virilio, is moreover a 'cyberwar' society, a post-Cold War society of the 'information bomb' or of 'information war'. The immediacy of information itself can create crises, according to Virilio, but what he has predicted is not particularly original, only

the way he has said it. The ideas themselves were formed in the
early Cold War period. In the 1950s the scientist Albert Einstein
had claimed the unfolding in the future of three kinds of 'bomb'.
These were: the atomic bomb, which had of course already been
dropped on Hiroshima and Nagasaki at the end of the Second
World War; the information bomb; and the population (or in
Virilio's words, the genetic) bomb. The second of these, the information bomb, where interactivity is created on a worldwide scale, is
what Virilio has concentrated on in his study of the society of the
accident. The 'second bomb', as well as the first, has been seen by
the German theorist Friedrich Kittler, in conversation with Paul
Virilio (1999b), as a long-term result of the Second World War. For
Kittler, with whom Virilio concurred in their fascinating if
rambling discussion, 'the truth is that both computers and atomic
bombs are an outcome of the Second World War'. Indeed, as Kittler
put it, 'nobody ordered them'. His view, with which Virilio agreed,
was that it was 'the strategic and military situation of the Second
World War that brought them into being ... they were not devised
as communication tools but as means of planning and conducting
total war'. The acceleration of the rate of information, especially as
a result of action by the US military machine (which was the basis
for the original setting-up of the internet, for example) has thus
produced the information bomb that Einstein warned the world of
the 1950s about. Virilio has agreed with another of his interlocutors
Philippe Petit that the 'military-industrial complex' is at the origin
of the internet. 'The internet is the product of the Pentagon and all
the satellite technologies were initially military', and in the process
they have achieved 'the militarisation of knowledge' rather than
simply the militarisation of science, Virilio has emphatically
reminded us. Virilio has noted too that 'the Pentagon's latest
technologies of war are virtual war technologies, information war
technologies', and that in his opinion war post-Vietnam 'has become
an essentially electronic phenomenon', a thesis he has applied in
analysing the 'Desert Screen' and 'war at the speed of light' in the
first Gulf War in the early 1990s. The spectre of Einstein's second
bomb is looming for Virilio at the beginning of the twenty-first
century. Dangerously, the information bomb is capable in his view
of using the 'interactivity of information to wreck the peace

between nations'. The internet literally has 'mail-bombing' campaigns where anyone can 'become a cyber-terrorist at little risk to themselves', and where there is a permanent temptation to engage in this new kind of war. In his most prophetic, at times hyper-provocative, statements Virilio even goes as far as to say that information war will actually replace 'traditional war' or industrial war.

In much of his work in the 1980s Virilio had already primed us to get used to this dangerous modernity implied by the information bomb in the idea of 'pure war'. For Virilio, the state of total peace is in actuality its opposite, what he conjures up in the phrase that became the title of Sylvère Lotringer's book of interviews with him: *Pure War*. In other words, in the implicit sense that Virilio means it, it is war pursued by other means. When war is ubiquitous, then we have the circumstances that Virilio has suggestively declaimed, one in which the 'military-industrial and scientific complexes continue to function on their own momentum'. Sometimes in Virilio's work this looks like the product of a deterministic 'economic' process rather like the cruder, simplistic materialist (neo-Marxist) versions of the 'military-industrial complex' produced in the postwar social sciences academy. On other occasions when Virilio speaks or writes of the military-industrial complex it seems to stem from a more complex set of conditions, and on yet others it has the imprint of some of the more fantastical conspiracy theories doing the rounds on the internet. Whatever our ultimate assessment of Virilio's interventions on this subject, it is clear that instead of Leon Trotsky's 'permanent revolution', Virilio has theorised 'permanent war'. World War III may not have taken place – or it may have, in the various outbreaks of military conflict since the minor 'Gulf War' between Iran and Iraq in the 1980s – but World War IV will always be with us! George W. Bush's notion after the attacks of 11 September 2001 of a 'war on terror' banner, headlined around the world by the US television news stations such as Fox and CNN, is a case in point. It is (information) war without (an) end. Virilio's friend Jean Baudrillard sees the theory of 'pure war' being pushed to its absolute limit in the oeuvre of Paul Virilio and gives approval to it as an idea:

The calculation of Paul is to push the military to a kind of extreme absolute of power that can ultimately only cause its own downfall, place it before the judgement of a God and absorb it into the society it destroys. He carries out this calculation with such an identification or obsession that I can credit him only with a powerful sense of irony: the system devours its own principle of reality, outbids on its own vacuous form until it attains to an absolute end or limit, to its ironical destiny of reversal. (Genosko 2001: 128)

We do not have to go as far as to equate Baudrillard's distinctive theoretical gaze with that of Virilio to recognise some of Virilio's own unique angle on the speeding-up of military technology and the speeding-up of modern, mediatised culture. Whether that vision holds together is interrogated later in this book and compared to Baudrillard's outrageously non-judgemental view of the simulated globe, rather than the real-and-virtual world conjured up by Paul Virilio.

Christianity, and specifically Virilio's Catholic anti-statism, is always lurking behind the theoretical implicitness of 'pure war'. Virilio himself has asserted that for 'God, history is a landscape of events. For Him, nothing really follows sequentially since everything is co-present', as if to underscore the sceptical (but admiring) interpretation of the non-believer Jean Baudrillard. Baudrillard himself certainly would be unlikely to quote approvingly from Ecclesiastes in the Bible as Virilio does on occasion. However, time – in Virilio's words, 'the collapse of time, the acceleration of time, the reversal of time, the simultaneity of all times' – unites, albeit temporarily, these two distinct thinkers, and helps to begin to explain what makes up some of the elements of dangerous modernity, a situation where, in Virilio's words, the 'history that is beginning is synchronised to world time, in other words, it's happening "live"'.

This is where the importance of the media, the mediation of events, comes into view so poignantly in Virilio's writings. For Jean Baudrillard there is not a positive word to say about the acceleration of history through the media. This is not the way his thinking proceeds. In contrast, accelerated temporality is not necessarily all bad in Virilio's view. A good example of what he means by the 'positive and accidental consequences' of the acceleration of events in the media was the 'live' release of Nelson Mandela from prison in South Africa after many years of incarceration by the apartheid regime. Virilio has noted that Mandela:

> was supposed to be freed at three o'clock in the afternoon and every television station in the world was there to witness his release from prison. However, this liberation was delayed. It was out of the question for these stations to give up and go off the air because no one knew when he was going to be released. So television was stuck in chronological time. It was no longer in the time of immediacy, since the time of Mandela's liberation was unknown and uncertainty reigned ... And during that half-hour they stayed there and waited for Mandela's release while watching young girls playing together and zooming on cars that were arriving but were empty etc. Television had become if not mute, then at least subjected to waiting. It was no longer in the event just taking place or that had just taken place, but rather in the anticipation of an event. So for once television was outside of this ocular drilling, this drilling of the gaze to immediacy which in some way represents an asphyxiation of the viewer's perception. (Virilio 1999: 86)

The mediation of the media is then a crucial and, sometimes as we have seen, positive dimension for Virilio in the acceleration of the landscape of events, or what we might also refer to, following commentators on Virilio, as 'mediated blitzes'.

News travels fast

In the mid to late 1990s another phase of Paul Virilio's publishing venture began, a phase which continues even today. Virilio retired from his post as Professor of Architecture at the Ecole Spéciale d'Architecture in the late 1990s ostensibly to write a book on the 'accident' (supposedly to be entitled in English *The Accident*), which he says he has actually been writing, at least in part, for ten years. It is certainly possible to argue that this project and all his published work, interviews and exhibitions since 1996 have been all of a piece. In fact, as we have seen, Virilio thinks all of his books do 'form a whole'. Virilio has also admitted that his books have always been 'written ... in series' though not 'deliberately', 'it just naturally works out that way', 'it's not a desire to write books, in fact it's events that set them off and running'. The problem is what might be chosen as an 'event' in a landscape where there are 'myriad incidents' and 'minute facts either overlooked or deliberately ignored'. Virilio has never actually given any cogent reason for choosing one event to write or talk about rather than another. It is unlikely that any systematic methodological reasoning could be found and, as we shall see later in this book, searches for socio-logical method or even any recognisable social science theory in Virilio's entire catalogue are likely to be very much in vain. But it is significant that the events he chooses to write or talk about illustrate the way that the past and future 'loom up together in all their simultaneity' and that they are heavily mediatised.

The events, or accidents, or mediated blitzes which set Virilio off and running seem to have come thick and fast in the last few years of the twentieth century and the first few years of the twenty-first century, suggesting that at least intuitively he has a finger on some pulse. Moreover, it is clear that these 'incidents' and 'accidents' are more than ever conveyed by an international media culture. What-ever else he is in these later years, Virilio is a theorist of accelerated media culture. But this is not the media theory of standardised media and communications studies in the arts, humanities and social science departments of the global academy for the last thirty years. We might, if we were mischievous, want to label this enter-prise in which Paul Virilio is engaged a 'history of the present'. Scholars who use this phrase, however, are more usually alluding to the body of work on governance and governmentality generated by the enquiries of Michel Foucault, and a number of his latter-day followers, in particular and, as we have already emphasised, Foucault's analyses are of a completely different order to those of Virilio. Nevertheless, the phrase does come up in association with the work of Virilio and he certainly believes that 'here no longer exists, everything is now'. In this role Virilio is writing an imme-diate account of the present where history has disappeared. Virilio is a 'presentist' if he is not an historian of the present. As he has admitted in interview:

> Since relativity, speed is absolute and is a limit on human activity. The loss of history means that the immediacy of the present prevails over the past and the future. So the possibility of a 'presentified'

history emerges, one known as current events or NEWS. There again is the considerable importance of the communication revolution and the power of the media. History only happens in the present. Today historians are being pushed around by the media. Everyone doing serious work in history must work on the media, except that this work has nothing to do with the old chronicler's work. Today's chronicles are predigested matter in which information is abridged as much as possible. History has been created through stories and the memories of individuals having witnessed certain events. Today, however, the media no longer exists as narratives but rather as flashes and images. History is therefore being reduced to images. (Virilio 1999: 57)

Accelerated and dangerous modernity are here being captured, idiosyncratically, by the 'presentism' of Virilio. Flashes and images have indeed replaced the narratives of more conventionally practised history.

The books and interviews in this period of the mid to late 1990s, as well as the mediated blitzes, also came thick and fast. Some of Virilio's logically clearest and most important work, and its explication in conversation, has definitively emerged in these latter years. In 1996 *Un Paysage d'Evénements* was published in the 'Collection L'Espace Critique' series. Later, an English translation, with the addition of a foreword by architect Bernard Tschumi, who had also contributed to the tenth-anniversary edition of Parent and Virilio's *Architecture Principe* in 1996, came out in 2000 in the Massachusetts Institute of Technology (MIT) 'Writing Architecture' series with the title of *A Landscape of Events* (Virilio 2000b). It was Tschumi who came up with the notion of 'mediated blitzes' which summarises Virilio's focus and subject matter so well. The book was a 'countdown' where he deliberately turned the clock back on the events of a period of twelve years. Virilio later told interviewer Sylvère Lotringer: 'I come to some conclusions about what has just happened in 1996 then we trace things backwards to 1984.' It was, in Virilio's words, a 'travelogue in time', composed backwards not chronologically 'so that you get an impression of shifting reality'. The sudden unfolding of time, the 'acceleration of the reality of time', has produced 'revulsion at the being-here-present' in Virilio's view. He revealed to Lotringer that he was:

pleased with the book, but it's more of an impressionistic work. It collapses twelve years in which absolutely everything happened. Between 1984 and 1996 we saw it all; not only the Berlin Wall, the implosion of the Soviet Union and the Gulf War, but also small microscopic events like Daboville's circumnavigation in a rowboat and the bombing of the World Trade Center etc. So it's a book that tries to show that eventual history broke down in favour of general history. General history is all about long stretches of time, and so Braudel, Bloch and the Ecoles des Annales are right, primacy has passed from general history to eventual history. Local time has won over. (Virilio 1997a: 166)

In fact, general history or the 'history of events' is no longer a tenable distinction for Virilio because the scale of 'values of the facts no longer allows simple discrimination between the general and the particular and the global and the local'. Virilio saw *A Landscape of Events* as 'halfway between an essay and a narrative in which atypical events succeed each other over the course of only a dozen years or so; events whose scope has escaped the theorists as much as the historians of the moment'. The next publication for Virilio, *Cybermonde, La Politique du Pire*, was a collection of interviews with Philippe Petit, a French journalist. It was published by Les Editions Textuel in Paris, again in 1996. Semiotext(e) published an English translation in 1999 under the title *Politics Of The Very Worst*. In 1997 Sylvère Lotringer conducted a new interview with Virilio, and in the same year Semiotext(e) reissued *Pure War* with the new interview as a 'Postscript'. A book of interviews with interlocutor Marianne Brausch entitled *Voyage d'Hiver* (Virilio 1997c) was also published in 1997 by Editions Parenthèses in Marseille. This interview book has not been translated in any form into English. In 1998 *La Bombe Informatique* was published in the 'Collection L'Espace Critique' series, and an English translation put out by Verso as *The Information Bomb* (Virilio 2000c) in 2000. Some of the essays in *The Information Bomb* were originally articles for German, Swiss and Austrian newspapers between 1996 and 1998. For Virilio, in this book which echoes the scientific theme explicitly in the title, the military and other relevant forces were seen to be developing the power of information in order to create a veritable weapon of world deterrence, that is the computer bomb or the information bomb first pointed to by scientist Albert Einstein. The book covered these and other processes including the genetic revolution and the question of whether there is a militarisation or civilianisation of science currently taking place. /

In 1999 *Stratégie de la Déception* was published in the 'Collection L'Espace Critique' series and an English translation was issued by Verso in 2000 as *Strategy of Deception*. *Strategy of Deception* was made up of three newspaper articles written during the Kosovo war between April and June 1999 and a fourth piece written in July 1999. The idea of 'deception' had a double meaning: 'disappoint-ment', which is the normal meaning of 'la déception' in French, but also the connotation of the deflection of military missiles from their course. Both ideas have significance for Virilio's discussion at the time of the NATO action in the former Yugoslavia at the end of the century of 'hyperviolence', which we are, in his view, better to 'forget'. In Virilio's eyes, the casualities were civilian in this new Balkan war unleashed in the name of human rights, while the military were protected as a species. The war in Kosovo, for Virilio, had zero deaths for the military but also zero victories in political terms. Alongside the humanitarian rhetoric of the avowed Christ-ians Tony Blair and Bill Clinton, there was evidence, according to Virilio, of a new form of war where territorial space was being displaced by orbital space, and air and space law continue to take precedence over law on the ownership and use of habitable land territory, a theme which Virilio often takes up in his later years. The 'humanitarian' and the 'military' strategies, for Virilio, are more and more integrally connected as in Kosovo. Moreover, in his view, a world society is forming which will try to regulate violence and war, to 'give it form':

> a new form of war is looming on a world scale that might be the beginning of the first real world war – because let me remind you that World War II was not truly a world war, no more than World War I. With the new technologies, the possibility to regulate or formalise a world war and to counter it with defense becomes a probability. This is a trend. Perhaps it will all come crashing down and degenerate into chaos, and then we can witness a global Yugoslavia. (Virilio 1999: 104–5)

According to Virilio, writing in the late 1990s, the war in Kosovo is giving way 'to a weapons ecosystem capable of setting off the chain reaction of a full scale cybernetic accident, in which disruption of the airwaves will predominate over the ravages caused by bombing'. In fact, the next total accident was in the US itself. Virilio had seen this coming too. In 1993 the first World Trade Center attack took place and Virilio wrote about it. He also wrote and spoke presciently in the intervening years about the coming terrain of an accident of accidents. As it turned out, the front of the new war, where accidents and attacks merge, occurred on 11 September 2001 and a more generalised era, where such accidents would occur more often, was ushered in. Indeed, in 1997 Virilio told Sylvère Lotringer, 'for my money, we have entered an age of large scale terrorism'. Within four years Virilio had been proved right in no uncertain terms, although in what Virilio has written around and about 11 September 2001 there is very little crowing. In 2002 he published in French *Ce Qui Arrive* (actually written in October 2001) with Editions Galilée, which was subsequently published in English translation as *Ground Zero* (Virilio 2002a) by Verso. It is an obtuse book which mentions 11 September 2001 as an event a couple of times only. We shall now take the opportunity to examine the 2001 World Trade Center attack as a kind of case-study event in order to look at the thrust of the generality of Paul Virilio's thinking on the accident specifically, and on speed, the accident, technology and modernity more generally, especially in relation to the 'communications revolution'.

Speed kills

On a bright, sunny morning on 11 September 2001 'the Manhattan skyline became the front of the new war', for Virilio writing about the event in *Ground Zero*. In a post-11 September interview with Sylvère Lotringer he has described the event even more explicitly as 'the dawn of a new war'. The events that took place that day are what citizens and media commentators in the USA have come to call, pervasively, '9/11', what Virilio labelled 'an act of total war'. They will not be forgotten for at least the rest of the century. The twin World Trade Center towers in Lower Manhattan, New York, were hit by Boeing 767 airliners flown into them seemingly deliberately by hijackers who had apparently boarded them at domestic American airports. In the widely-disseminated official version of events it is probable that only the hijackers who flew the planes on their short flights on the East Coast of the USA knew of their ultimate objective and that the passengers on board were unaware of their terrible fate until the very last moment. The North tower of the World Trade Center was hit by a Boeing 767 travelling at 440 miles per hour, and some cameras caught the moment of impact itself. The plane, with many passengers on board and huge supplies of aviation fuel, ploughed into the North tower between the ninety-third and ninety-eighth floor of the 105-storey building. Its engines slammed fast into the inner core of the skyscraper. Fire started immediately. The aviation fuel spread the fire so fast that it effectively cut the building in two. Approximately 1,000 people were trapped above the ninty-eighth floor. About twenty minutes later another Boeing 767 travelling at similar speeds slammed into the South tower. It had also seemingly been hijacked and flown deliberately into the World Trade Center. The South tower was hit between the seventy-eighth and eighty-fourth floors. The second plane missed most of the inner core of the building and started fires at the perimeter. The South tower completely collapsed after the fires had burned so fiercely that the steel melted. Virilio has noted in interview with Sylvère Lotringer that 'it was amazing … that the Twin Towers withstood the impact' for so long, allowing many people to escape. For Virilio the firefighters were 'the real heroes' and it was 'a miracle that the two buildings stood as long as they did'. 'Under normal circumstances', Virilio claimed, 'the impact and the fire should have taken down the tower in fifteen minutes … had the towers been knocked down, there would have been forty thousand dead in one blow'. Survivors who had escaped to the street below described the scene after the collapse of the tower as 'like a nuclear winter'. The South tower, when it did eventually succumb to the fire, in fact took only thirty seconds to collapse into the streets below. Twenty-five minutes later the North tower also collapsed. Altogether just under 3,000 people probably died at the World Trade Center towers, including 479 emergency service workers and 157 people aboard the two hijacked passenger airliners which crashed into the towers. From the time shortly before the second plane hit, the attack was captured 'live' on television and relayed 'live' all around the world. Billions of people in hundreds of countries watched at exactly the same time on millions of screens as the spectacular events unfolded like those of a cinematic film. There was immense confusion among the commentators as news quickly filtered through that the Pentagon had apparently suffered a similar direct hit by a hijacked passenger aircraft (although subversive counter-arguments later alleged a missile attack). The fire damage caused was shown a few minutes later by television cameras. A fourth plane, hijacked to Pennsylvania with an unknown destination, crashed. No television camera recorded the events involving the flights of the third or fourth planes. The media outcome of the event was that the architectural symbols of American capitalism, not to mention the military control centre, had been destroyed, with huge loss of life, in a matter of a couple of hours as billions of citizens of the world watched 'live', real-time television with shock, alarm and incredulity.

The spectacular and tragic attack on the World Trade Center and the simultaneous attack on the Pentagon in Washington on 11 September 2001 was an example of what Virilio meant throughout the 1990s in his writings and interviews when he was conjuring up the society of the accident and in particular the coming of a period of the accident of accidents, a more widespread total accident or general accident. It is also an instance of what is implied by the term dangerous modernity as a concept stemming from the analysis in this book of Virilio's rhetorical discourse and hundreds of anecdotal suggestions. In fact, the World Trade Center in New York was first attacked over eight years previously by a small group planting a bomb on 26 February 1993 killing six people and injuring over 1,000 others. Virilio wrote about the 1993 event in a piece written at the time but published in France in 1996 in *Un Paysage d'Evénements* and eventually published in English in 2000 in the book *A Landscape of Events*. As Virilio showed in his pithy essay, one single, yellow Ford van, hired from Ryder, containing a 1,200-pound bomb, did the damage and may have brought down one of the towers altogether if it had been planted in a slightly different place. Paul Virilio was even engaged as a consultant by

American authorities after the 1993 event. It may seem bizarre for a liberal or left-leaning intellectual to be hired by more neo-conservative foes but it has occasionally happened to Virilio over his career. Although military chiefs have often disagreed with his analyses of military attacks and technological change, he has been sought out by the military. Moreover, his views on the aspects of a legal system necessary to mete out justice in such cases as the 1993 attack, which he predicted would escalate at a pace over the coming years, are clear and unequivocal. They would not necessarily have upset the military and political establishments in their formal legalism. After the 1993 World Trade Center event Virilio said:

> At the very moment that the United Nations is hoping to re-establish an international tribunal to try the authors of war crimes, it is equally urgent to severely punish terrorist practices, no matter what their source; otherwise we will look on, powerless, as this type of 'economical' operation suddenly proliferates, capable as it is of inflicting incredible damage not only on the innocent victims but also, and especially, on democracy. (Virilio 2000b: 19)

Virilio's occasional consultancy work, however, is perhaps less important than his uncannily accurate predictions about what was to follow 1993. The 'miniaturisation of charges' and 'advances in the chemistry of detonation' which Virilio mentioned in his acute analysis of the World Trade Centre attack of 1993 did, in reality, make the 2001 spectacular event even more inevitable. Further, in the *Pure War* 'Postscript' interview with Sylvère Lotringer in 1997 (subtitled 'Infowar') Virilio recalled the World Trade Center 'event' or 'accident' of 1993 and reflected upon its significance with chilling foresight. He proclaimed (speaking of the early 1990s) that indeed 'we have entered an age of large scale terrorism':

> The World Trade Center was an initial indication of this, a kind of Hiroshima. Don't forget: the WTC bomb is just like Hiroshima and this takes us to the next stage. Oklahoma followed suit. Terrorist deaths used to be counted in their hundreds, now suddenly it could jump to 20,000 dead. I was asked to investigate the WTC blast. If the van had managed to park at the base of the tower, instead of the access ramp, the whole Trade Center would have gone up. In what way we can't imagine. But there would have been 10,000, 20,000 dead, in other words the equivalent of a strategic cruise missile

strike. The Iraqi war didn't go that far. Ten to twenty thousand deaths is the equivalent of a full-scale military operation. A mere five men and a van, but a well-positioned van would have done it. (Virilio 1997a: 170–1)

In the final analysis of the official version of '9/11', it took nineteen men and a few boxcutters to destroy the towers in 2001. Sylvère Lotringer, in the extra interview, included in the 1997 interviews, stressed that the idea of 'pure war' which Virilio had initially put forward in the Lotringer/Semiotext(e) interviews of 1982 'seems as though it's even more the order of the day than it was fifteen years ago'. Virilio himself agreed that 'it certainly is the order of the day ... [i]t's a crazy engine that won't stop'. Lotringer queried the example of the 1993 World Trade Center case because, in his view, it 'wasn't even a nuclear threat, or an acceleration of speed'. In fact, although Virilio has never alluded to it, it could be said that speed *was* the essence of war in this scenario. The bomb made by Ramzi Yousef, the main protagonist in the 1993 attack, was constructed for its high speed. Normally, high explosives have a velocity of 3,000ft per second. Yousef and his group's attack on the World Trade Center basement, aiming to blow up one tower which would then collapse into the other, used a bomb with a velocity of more than 15,000ft per second, at least five times the normal speed. In response to Lotringer, however, Paul Virilio answered very succinctly about the speed of the media and the 'live' nature of broadcasting in the city of the instant:

Terrorism uses the speed of mass communication. Let's remind ourselves that terrorism needs the media. If you manage to blow up the WTC without anyone knowing about it, that's pointless. The same goes for 10,000 dead and no one batting an eyelid. The problem is that two people are killed in Somalia and they happen to be Americans, it's a national drama. You see that terrorism anticipated the information war described by the Pentagon, which is now preparing a revolution in military matters based on infowar and the infosphere. The first to have waged such an information war were the terrorists. They scheduled their bomb-blast on time to catch the evening news. The explosion only exists because it is simultaneously coupled to a multimedia explosion. What is more, the WTC is a teleport, a communications centre. An economic and communications centre. (Virilio 1997a: 174)

The speed of mass communication therefore is crucial according to Virilio, and it certainly was critical to the event of 11 September 2001. What Virilio sees as the communications revolution has, in general, been crucial for the shift in gear of international 'terror' attacks. It is now the internet, Global Positioning Satellites (or GPS) and mobile communications which give small, committed groups more power than the nation state itself had only a few decades, or even a few years, ago. What Virilio was really probing in his musings on the Ramzi Yousef cell's World Trade Center attack of February 1993, which he was asked to investigate, is the more general notion of an 'information accident', one which 'simultane-ously happened everywhere': in other words, an 'information panic'. As Lotringer, Virilio's interlocutor, put it, still skating over the speed of the bomb as if that did not matter at all: 'it's not the power of the explosion itself but the media explosion that matters'. Once again, however, the simultaneity and ubiquity (which are Virilio's major themes) of the attack itself should not be under-estimated. After his attack on the World Trade Center, Ramzi Yousef allegedly planned, with others, later in the mid 1990s, to bomb out of the sky eleven passenger airliners at the same time. The 11 September 2001 attack on the World Trade Center and the Pentagon (and at least one other unnamed target, possibly the White House) witnessed at least two airliners hit their targets within a few minutes of each other, a third perhaps 'disappear', and a fourth crash occur shortly afterwards. It is estimated by some commentators that up to eight airliners were to be used as weapons of attack at almost the same time, but the grounding of all air traffic in the wake of the two airliners hitting the World Trade Center meant several hijacks being aborted. The effect of the simultaneous 'accident' of September 2001 was undoubtedly to affect 'every-where', as Virilio has suggested the 'accident of accidents' will do.

The P.V.

In the context of the example of 11 September 2001, it is of some importance that Paul Virilio has written in detail on the original 1993 World Trade Center bomb as a defining moment. It is only one essay contained in Virilio's *A Landscape of Events*, the series of essays originally written between 1984 and 1996, but it is a major one. In English the essay is entitled 'Delirious New York'. It is a more sustained essay than some of the others in the backward-looking collection, although it is still relatively short, and concentrates on prising open the significance of the 1993 World Trade Center 'event' or 'accident'. Written on 30 March 1993, 'Delirious New York' (or 'New York Délire' in the original French edition of *Un Paysage d'Evénements*) is a fascinating short piece of polemic given the spectacular subsequent attack on the World Trade Center on 11 September 2001, which itself pre-empted and ushered into being the US-proclaimed 'war on terrorism'. 'September 11' did indeed bring down the two towers with an estimated casualty toll of almost 3,000 people dead, all 'shot' live by television and transmitted simultaneously across the world. As Bernard Tschumi claims, in the special Foreword to the English edition of *A Landscape of Events*, the theoretical context for an essay on the World Trade Center event (or the Gulf War, or the fiftieth anniversary of D-Day, or whatever other event Virilio looked into in the book) is that, as a theorist, Virilio analyses 'global temporal space'. Tschumi says that Virilio focuses on 'the acceleration' of 'temporal reality' where an 'event' is a 'kind of accident'. In Tschumi's view, for Virilio:

> Each collision is an event relayed by media – political, social, technological. No value judgements here: after all, an event is a kind of accident, one that arises from the unlikely collision of generally uncoordinated vectors. Accidents will happen. Conveyed by media culture, P.V.'s events are less here than now. His definition of the event is less in space than in time. P.V.'s thesis may be simply that time has finally overcome space as our main mode of perception. (Virilio 2000b: ix)

Bernard Tschumi, writing in English in an introduction to an English translation of essays originally in French, takes great delight in pointing out that in French 'P.V.' (procès-verbal) also means – apart from being the initials of Paul Virilio – 'an official report, a journal, the minutes of a proceeding, a police report, even a parking or speeding ticket'. For Tschumi, P.V. writes P.V. In other words, Virilio reports on incidents and occurrences like the World Trade Center bomb of 1993, but in such a way that the theory of the society of the accident, or dangerous modernity, always underpins such reports and goes to the heart of 'major trans-formations in today's society'. For Tschumi, these are P.V.'s times for sure. But there are many other public intellectuals than Paul Virilio. They, too, have written about events such as 11 September 2001.

It is interesting to contrast Virilio in this context with someone against whom critics measure him: Noam Chomsky. Chomsky published only a few weeks after the incident (à la Virilio) a short book of interviews called *September 11* (Chomsky 2001) about the implications of the attacks. In the interviews with various journalists in the book, Chomsky is strongly critical of what he describes as US state 'terrorist' activity of its own over the years in places such as El Salvador or Nicaragua. He also points to the fact that 'the horrifying atrocities of 11 September are something quite new in world affairs' because 'this is the first time since the war of 1812 that the national territory has been under attack, or even threatened'. However, there is little of the re-theorising of the events which might be found in a similar book by Paul Virilio. There is no sense from reading Chomsky that it is the accelerating media culture which makes the 'event' or 'accident' so significant, which is what a Virilio 'look' at the subject would emphasise. This gap is the biggest difference between the two thinkers. Chomsky is content to make fairly standard political-science arguments which could have been made in the USA at any time in the last fifty years, although his critical warnings to the George W. Bush administration and security services were telling, even in the short period before the American allied attacks on Afghanistan and even more so after the vanquishing of the Taliban. Moreover, few liberal critics in the USA, beyond a literary figure like Gore Vidal, are brave enough to say any more what Chomsky is prepared to say. In truth, the political positions of Virilio and Chomsky are probably not so different from each other. Both are left-liberal humanist critics prepared to speak out as public intellectuals critical of the military and political strategies of the West.

Un homme – une guerre totale

In his 1993 World Trade Center bomb essay, in an uncannily prescient foretaste of what was apparently to come eight years later,

Virilio talked of the possibility of 'One Man = Total War'. This was the translation of the phrase *'un homme – une guerre totale'* in the original French in the 'Delirious New York' essay in *A Landscape of Events*. By 2001, even though his presence as a thorn in the side of America had been well known for more than a decade, Saudi dissident, and former fighter in the Afghan war with the Soviet Union in the 1980s, Osama bin Laden fitted Virilio's description like a glove. President George W. Bush's 'chief suspect' after the 2001 attack and public enemy number one in the 'war on terrorism', he matched the idea of the West at war with 'One Man' put forward by Virilio in 1993. However, the most noteworthy issue is that Virilio in his essay directly pointed to the actual carrying-out of large-scale attack by minimalist means. He argued that 'it has reached the point where soon, if we don't look out, a single man may well be able to bring about disasters that were once, not long ago, the province of a naval or air force squadron'. However loosely his al-Qaeda organisation was involved in the 11 September 2001 attacks, it is argued in the official version that Osama bin Laden was the identikit picture of that 'single man'.

Minimalism was what mattered in Virilio's predicted scenario because of the changes in speed and technology, and in particular in communications throughout the globe, which shrink the planet. For Virilio commenting on the 1993 event at the time, the only requirements for *'un homme – une guerre totale'* were twofold. First, a 'limited number of actors'. In the 2001 case, taking at face value the official evidence in the public arena, probably fewer than nineteen men hijacked four domestic airliners in the USA and crashed at least two of them, with devastating effect in terms of human casualties, into the World Trade Center causing huge fires and the eventual collapse of the skyscrapers. Second, a 'guaranteed media coverage'. 'Live' footage of the second plane hitting the South tower of the World Trade Center and the subsequent terrifying collapse of both the North and South towers (structures which were architecturally designed to withstand an 'accident' like passenger planes crashing into them) were shown on prime-time television around the world as the famous New York skyline changed in a matter of minutes before billions of watchers' eyes. In the case of the 1993 event, the plot eventually resulted in the imprisonment of the chief suspect, Ramzi Yousef. Yousef was a self-confessed 'terrorist' trained in Osama bin Laden camps in Afghanistan, who again fitted the *'un homme – une guerre totale'* formula at the time of the plan to bring down the major 'economic nerve centre' and one of the tallest buildings in the world in the heart of Manhattan, in front of a live television audience of billions of people. This 1993 event, for Virilio, was a project 'involving only a small number of individuals who used a delivery van to deliver terror'. 'In the days of cruise missiles and the most sophisticated nuclear weapons carriers', Virilio joked with gallows humour that 'you have to admit that this is a striking example of political economy'.

In September 2001 Virilio's earlier prophecy appeared to come tragically true as a small, tightly-knit group of men, armed only with boxcutters, were said to have taken over the cockpits of the hijacked planes and flown jet airliners with large amounts of fuel into the highly populated buildings of the World Trade Center. The beginning of this post-Cold War 'age of imbalance', as Virilio has called it, was as he said at the time of the 1993 event:

> In the manner of a massive aerial bombardment, this single bomb, made of several hundred kilos of explosives placed at the building's very foundations, could have caused the collapse of a tower 400 metres high. So it is not a simple remake of the film *Towering Inferno*, as the age-conscious media like to keep saying, but much more of a strategic event confirming for us all The Change In The Military Order Of This Fin-De-Siècle. As the bombs of Hiroshima and Nagasaki, in their day, signalled a new era for war, the explosive van in New York illustrates the mutation of terrorism. (Virilio 2000b: 18)

Virilio noted at the time of the 1993 event that the perpetrators of such acts 'are determined not merely to settle the argument with guns' but will 'try to devastate the major cities of the world marketplace'. Within eight years a small group of determined men had indeed apparently done so. Many of the features of what Virilio set out in the essay in 1993 as being on the cards for the future of humanity were to be put into practice with exactly this effect of the 'devastation' of a world city.

The museum of accidents

In fact, ironically, 'towering inferno' images probably were rife in the minds of many of the watchers of the 2001 'event' or 'accident'. In Virilio's book *Ground Zero*, he has explicitly claimed that as the twin towers attack was being 'broadcast live many TV viewers believed they were watching one of those disaster movies that proliferate endlessly on our TV screens' and that it was only 'by switching channels and finding the same pictures on all the stations that they finally understood that it was true'. Aesthetically '9/11' was taken as an 'art of terrorism' in some quarters. Virilio quotes the avant-garde electronic composer Karlheinz Stockhausen as saying it was 'the greatest work of art there has ever been'. The Brit-artist Damien Hirst also claimed that those responsible for the attack should indeed be congratulated because they achieved 'something which nobody would ever have thought possible' on an artistic level. The event was, in Hirst's view, 'kind of like an artwork in its own right ... wicked, but it was devised in this way for this kind of impact' and 'was devised visually'. But by the beginning of the new century it was the visual art of computer games which probably had most resonance, at least amongst the younger citizens of the 'collective world city' who were glued to their television screens on 11 September 2001. Remarkably, a Microsoft Flight Simulator 2000 computer game, which some feared had been used by the hijackers of the planes, at least in part, to practise for their suicide mission, was on sale at the time of the event, retailing in high-street stores at about $80. It was withdrawn rapidly in the wake of the information panic after 11 September but its basic programme included the capacity of would-be pilots to pretend to crash Boeing 757s and 767s (the planes used in the actual attack) into the World Trade Center. The graphic images in the game of planes embedded in the higher parts of the towers were uncannily like the moment of impact of the hijacked planes flying into the World Trade Center captured live on television. It is thought by some investigators that the hijackers who flew the planes into the World Trade Center on 11 September had indeed learned to do so on such simulation systems because of their closeness to 'reality'. In another game, WTC Defender, also quickly withdrawn after the September 2001 event, players could pretend to shoot down pilots as they attacked the World Trade Center. If an aircraft got through, the buildings blew up. The game had been available to download over the internet.

The links between such 'new media' (computer games) and the events which Virilio has written about (the 1993 World Trade Center attack, for instance) is obviously of fascination and interest given his consistent focus on war, cinema and photography and our consideration of the significance of 11 September 2001 for assessing Virilio's notion of the accident. But for Virilio, unlike other French theorists of mass culture such as Gilles Deleuze, 'cinema and television have nothing in common'. Virilio has argued the case that 'video technologies and technologies of simulation have been used for war'. For Virilio, 'video was created after the Second World War in order to radio control planes and aircraft carriers' In fact, Virilio has argued that 'video came with the war (and) took twenty years before it became a means of expression for artists'. However, Virilio has also noted that it is 'television' which is 'the actual museum of accidents'. For years he has been reportedly planning a 'museum of the accident' in Japan, for so long the home of the new technologies of the media. For Virilio, its 'art is to be the site where all accidents happen. But that is its only art'. Television has, for Virilio, already died:

> I would say that television is already dead with the advent of multimedia. It is clear that interactivity is the end of television. I would like to say that the example of television is already outdated. Just as photography gave rise to cinematography, video and television are today giving rise to infography. Television is already a surviving form of media. (Virilio 1999: 46)

The 'museum of accidents' certainly preserved for posterity the attacks of 11 September 2001 and enabled us to make the case study we have used in this chapter to look at Virilio's thinking on the accident, but Virilio has already started to give up on television as a cultural form. He has gone on record as saying that:

> I think that the drilling of the gaze by television has gone so far that it is no longer possible to straighten out the situation in one hour. That being said, I am not opposed to showing catastrophes or

accidents, because I believe a museum of accidents is necessary. (On this subject, remember that the tape of the Rodney King affair has been put in a museum.) However, I think that television has become the advertising or propaganda medium par excellence. We saw this during the Gulf War, with Timisoara, and we see it every day. Honestly, I am beginning to give up on television. I can no longer tolerate this kind of drilling. It would take the invention of another kind of television, but I believe it's too late. I think that there will be innovation with the new medium but not in the old one. The old medium has gone all the way to the end, which is to say to ITS end. In my opinion television is gone, but not video. (Virilio 1999: 47)

So, for Virilio, the 'accident museum exists'. He claims to 'have come across it: it is a TV screen', even if this particular form of technology is on the way out. The requirement of the accident, as 11 September 2001 showed only too well, is the urgency of the screening of the phases of the event live. Television certainly still fulfills this requirement.

For Virilio, however, what really counts is not so much the technology itself but the need to show 'fallibilism' in scientific and technological development in dangerous modernity. His demand is to 'go beyond an ideology of progress, linear and interrupted, excluding the importance of the mishap or the beneficial mistake'. To expose the accident, to exhibit the accident, in this museum of accidents for Virilio, then, is to 'expose the unlikely, to expose the unusual and yet inevitable' in recognising the 'symmetry between substance and accident'. The 'accident museum' is necessary, for Virilio, to preserve the collapsing buildings, high-speed plane crashes and other accidents of accelerated and dangerous modernity. Virilio, true to his word, jettisoned the televisual form and settled for the art gallery in his quest to preserve 11 September 2001 and hundreds of other disasters for the museum of accidents. A little over a year after '9/11' Virilio helped to create its first concrete realisation in a major French contemporary art exhibition entitled 'Ce Qui Arrive', translated as *Unknown Quantity* in the English version of the catalogue. This included diverse textual commentary on the theory of the accident by Virilio (Virilio 2003b) as well as beautifully presented photographs. Virilio curated the exhibition with a number of other artists at the Fondation Cartier pour l'Art

Contemporain in Paris, which opened in November 2002 and explicitly incorporated photographic, video and cinematic material from '9/11'. Virilio in the main provided the concepts for this pioneering art exhibition while curator Leanne Sacramone mapped them onto a series of artworks. As an addition to the catalogue of the exhibition, Virilio interviewed Svetlana Aleksievich, the author of a book about Chernobyl victims and witnesses. Virilio's emerging ideas on the accident formed the text of the catalogue's long introduction, under subheadings such as: the invention of accidents; the accident thesis; the museum of accidents; the future of the accident; the horizon of expectation and the unknown quantity. According to one commentator (Patrick 2003) on the exhibition, 'as war between nation states gives way to the less defined area of international terrorism, so the distinction between acts of war, man made accidents and natural disasters becomes less distinguishable'. This situation 'in turn leads to a panorama in which acts of God and events such as Chernobyl and 11 September together occupy an undifferentiated position at the centre of the world stage'. The museum of accidents, then, in this context is a twenty-first-century 'equivalent to the traditional war memorial's "lest we forget"'.

CHAPTER FOUR

Critical modernity

The 'art of the accident' as well as the 'museum of accidents' has been in Paul Virilio's sights as his work has developed over the years. The accident, for Virilio, is 'to the social sciences what sin is to human nature'. That is why he has argued that just as at the end of the nineteenth century museums exhibited machines, so in our age 'we must grant the formative dimension of the accident its rightful place in a new museum' and 'exhibit – I don't know how yet – train derailments, pollution, collapsed buildings'. So next to the 'hall of machines' we should put a 'hall of accidents', according to Virilio. The catalogue to the exhibition of the museum of accidents, *Unknown Quantity*, written by Paul Virilio, makes it clear that ten years after after his original Fondation Cartier pour l'Art Contemporain exhibition on speed, entitled 'La Vitesse' and organised at Jouy-en-Josas, the aim of the twenty-first-century collaboration with the Fondation Cartier in Paris was to create a 'pilot project for, or more exactly a prefiguration of, the future museum of the accident'. Thus, a 'landscape of events' in Virilio's vision would replace the former exhibition hall. Since the late 1980s Virilio has more or less consistently been engaged in 'surfing the accident', or studying the 'art of the accident'. As we have seen in the previous two chapters, we can understand Virilio's ideas on speed, technology and modernity and the notion of the accident with greater clarity if we introduce the concepts of accelerated modernity and dangerous modernity to the discussion. However, these concepts, even if they were even necessary, are certainly not sufficient to map the work that Virilio has done throughout his entire career. In this chapter we introduce the idea of 'critical modernity' which helps to situate 'the art', or the 'aesthetic', in the art of the accident in Virilio's wide-ranging writings. The interest in the art of the accident follows on for Virilio from the idea of the 'art of war' invented by his mentor Sun Tsu, original author of the 'essence of war is speed' motif so influential on Paul Virilio's life and work.

The art of war

At least one of Virilio's myriad interpreters has written of Virilio's 'accelerated aesthetics' (Armitage 1997). In general too, Virilio's partial legacy to a younger generation of intellectuals at the end of the twentieth century was very much an aesthetic and artistic cultural politics which fitted the spirit of the age, dominated by debates about postmodernism and postmodernity. Virilio's work in this area is in fragments to be sure, but substantial nonetheless. However, there is probably no reason to bracket Virilio with postmodern, or for that matter post-structuralist, theorists at all in assessing this aesthetic and cultural politics. Of all the French theorists discussed in this context in the international academy (Silverman 1999), Paul Virilio is probably the least appropriate choice. As he constantly reminds us he is interested in speed and war, and the politics associated with this, not postmodernism. Yet undoubtedly any consideration of postmodern culture depends on the accelerated culture, the accelerated modernity, and dangerous modernity, which this book has explicated in the work of the high priest of speed, Paul Virilio.

Virilio's writing and conversation has often ranged over different cultural forms and cultural personalities. Besides the major books, articles and interviews which have already featured in this book, there are many other publications by Virilio, either written jointly with others or single-authored, on the likes of the architect Jean Nouvel, the filmmaker Atom Egoyan, the artist Peter Klasen, the performance artist Stelarc, technological innovations in cinema such as the 1,000sq m hemispheric Géode cinema screen at Cité des Sciences at La Villette in France (Virilio 1990b), and subjects as diverse as dance, photography, posters, television, contemporary art, architecture, the desert and cinema. Virilio, however, has labelled himself a critic not of art per se but of the 'art of technology'. He has often used this stance to explain himself to non-believers:

> When someone says to me I don't understand your position, my response is, I'll explain it to you: I am a critic of the art of technology. Fair enough? That's all. If they still don't understand, then I say: just look at what an art critic is to traditional art, and then substitute technology for traditional art, and then you have my position. It's that simple. (Virilio 1997a: 172)

Crucially for a theorist of technology, Virilio has argued in interview with Louise Wilson that all 'technology has become art':

This is the art of the engine. Art used to be painting, sculpture, music etc but now all technology is art. Of course, this form of art is still very primitive, but it is slowly replacing reality. This is what I call the art of the engine. For instance, when I take the TGV (Train à Grande Vitesse) in France, I love watching the landscape: this landscape, as well as works by Picasso or Klee, is art. The engine makes the art of the engine. Wim Wenders made road movies, but what is the engine of a road movie. It's a car, like in *Paris Texas*. Dromoscopy. Now all we have to do to enter the realm of art is to take a car. (1994)

And, of course, for Virilio, in tracing the accelerating technologically-driven war of modernity, the 'landscape of war' has become cinematic. Virilio invented the term 'dromoscopy' (Virilio 1978) in the 1970s to characterise the effect of speed on the landscape, which in Virilio's case invariably means a military space. The cinema is war pursued by other means as Sylvère Lotringer has expressed it in his interpretations of the conversations with Virilio. But this is because, for Virilio, 'all speed illuminates'. In Virilio's words:

The world becomes a cinema. It's this effect of speed on the landscape that I called a Dromoscopy, in the strict sense. We speak of stroboscopy, in other words the effects induced by an energy and a relation of observation on an object. But this stroboscopy is also a dromoscopy. What happens in the train window, in the car windshield, in the television screen is the same kind of cinematism. We have gone from the aesthetics of appearance, stable forms, to the aesthetics of disappearance, unstable forms. (Virilio 1997a: 85)

'Appearance or disappearance, it's all sleight of hand, it's what happens in the movies', Virilio has pronounced in one of his aphoristic replies in interview. For him, cinematic images, in contrast to the painter's painting, are present only as far as they vanish quickly, flashing by at twenty-four images per second, and there are, as he points out, machines which go to a million images per second, reducing our vision to nothing, to blindness.

The idea of changes in speed and changes in representation that Virilio pursues over time is an important one, too. This idea constantly draws Virilio, as always, back to the Second World War:

It is well known that the war of 1939–1945 was a war of radio and cinema. It was a war of aviation and tanks, the Blitzkrieg of the

tanks invading France, the destruction of Coventry and Rotterdam
... But it was also Goebbels's frenzied use of the cinema and radio,
which he completely controlled, as well as the use of the latter by
the Resistance ... On the one hand, Hitler commanded his generals
and his troops by radio-telephone, while on the other he led his
people with radio and newsreels. People don't realise how much
newsreels ... are the same as the evening news on television. That is
where politics is played out. Before the fictional film, there were
newsreels in which the great Conducatore, Mussolini, and the
Führer both spoke. This is also what appears in theatrical political
ceremonies, such as the one in Nuremberg which, before even
becoming a propaganda film, was filmed theatre, an aesthetic way
to do politics ... Film then became a battle site. (Virilio 1999: 27–8)

Although much of what Virilio writes about war and cinema is
governed by his interest in the 'aesthetics' of disappearance, he is
well aware that people literally 'disappeared' in the fascist, and for
that matter Stalinist, regimes of the 1930s, not to mention in
Middle-Eastern and South-American dictatorships and as a result
of the activities of the secret police in civilian 'modern' societies
today. He has conceded that there are 'qualitative differences'
between people vanishing into thin air and the 'disappearance' as
the effect of broadcasting or the cinema:

This phenomenon nonetheless sheds light on terrorist practices as
well as on the state terrorism that developed in South America with
the technique of disappearances. No longer the practice of the
concentration camps, of German-style enclosure, but the disappearance of people. Sleight of hand. Social magic. It's the society of
disappearance. Until the Second World War – until the concentration camps – societies were societies of incarceration, of imprisonment in the Foucauldian sense. The great transparency of the
world, whether through satellites or simply tourists, brought about
an overexposure of these places to observation, to the press and
public opinion which now ban concentration camps. You can't
isolate anything in this world of ubiquity and instantaneousness.
Even if some camps do still exist, this overexposure of the world led
to the need to surpass enclosure and imprisonment. This required
the promotion of another kind of repression, which is
disappearance. (Virilio 1997a: 89)

The art of war in modernity for Virilio then has various implications, not just the question of how changes in ways of seeing
(cinema, television, video, photography) are produced by changes
in warfare and military practice. It seems sometimes that the
aesthetics of war for Virilio are inevitably going to be bound up in a
process of technological determinism, but there is more complexity
to Virilio than a simple reductionism.

Past the 'post' theory

Virilio's attachment to modernity, it can be argued, is specifically
framed by the 1939–45 conflict, which he experienced first-hand.
But some time in the aftermath of the Second World War the
existence and implications of what many contemporary theorists
have labelled as the 'postmodern' started to become discussed in
academic circles, especially in the fields of art and architecture. As
we have seen already, Virilio has bluntly decried the application of
the term in these fields. Although it had been introduced as a term
earlier in the postwar period, by the 1970s when Paul Virilio was in
the original stages of his academic career in the Special School of
Architecture in Paris, the phrase postmodernism had acquired a
certain currency, not least in his own chosen field of architecture.
However, it was not until the 1980s that the international academy,
and cultural journalism, debated and promoted it en masse. Virilio
in the 1980s embraced the notion of 'post-politics' put forward by
Semiotext(e) and the Italian Autonomists but this, for him, manifestly had nothing to do with debates about postmodernism.
Indeed, the most misleading critical analysis of Virilio is the
relatively common one that has placed him as a prominent figure in
the list of 'postmodern' philosophers. Sokal and Bricmont, in the
ill-judged *Intellectual Impostures*, were simply wrong in the present author's judgement to categorise him in this fashion, whatever
they may have thought of Virilio's use of natural science in his
work. Arguably, neither term, 'philosopher' nor 'postmodern', is
accurate or appropriate in Virilio's case. From time to time Virilio
has emphatically denied that he is a 'philosopher' at all, although
he has been called everything from a 'philosopher of space' to a
'philosopher of time' in his career. Moreover, to publicly distinguish

himself from philosophy proper he has noted in interview that the likes of Paul Ricoeur and Gilles Deleuze deserve the description 'philosophers'.

In terms of general categorisations, Virilio has accepted the self-proclaimed label 'urbanist' and also more bizarrely 'citizen of the world'. He has even on occasions proclaimed the 'end of geography', and then retracted the belief. He perhaps belongs, on these measures and on this evidence, in the company of 'postmodern geographers' like Edward Soja or David Harvey. But this is not an especially good comparison either. However, Virilio certainly puts the city at the centre of his thinking even if he does not see it in the postmodern philosopher's or geographer's terms. He has, for instance, proclaimed:

> Without the city, there can be no politics. Without the history of the city, there is no reality of history. The city is the major political form of history. My work deals not only with the narrative, but also with the trajectory … I do not work on the subject and object – that is the work of the philosopher – but rather on the 'traject'. I have even proposed to inscribe the trajectory between the subject and the object to create the neologism 'trajective', in addition to 'subjective' and 'objective'. I am thus a man of the trajective, and the city is the site of trajectories and trajectivity. (Virilio 1999: 40)

So the more accurate self-description of Virilio might not involve any of the conventional labels attributed to him at all. Nevertheless, in straightforward topological or geographical terms, Virilio has always been concerned with the fate of the city, and by implication the 'virtual city'. He has written and mused extensively in the later years of his life about the question of whether there will be a 'cyber city'. He has, for example, noted that:

> it is the entire city that is falling into the virtual and taking with it individuals who are getting ready to live there. The city has always been a theatrical device with the agora, the church, the forum, the parade ground etc. Simply put it was a place where you could gather together, a public space. Today, however, the television setting is replacing public space with public image, and the public image is decentred from the city. The public image is no longer in the city, but rather in the 'tele-citta' already a virtual city, in which we claim to co-habitate because we watch the evening news

together. I believe that what is in question behind the problem of virtual space is the loss of the real city. I am an urbanist, and for me, the real city is the site of the social body, the populating site … a sort of city of cities is being created: the telecommunications city, the internet city. Next to the virtual bubble of market economy, generated by the trading programme and by automatic stock quotations, a virtual urban bubble is forming in which public space has been definitively supplanted by public image. The propaganda about the internet and the information superhighway aims to urbanise real time at a time when real space is being deurbanised. (Virilio 1999: 45)

In making this kind of statement and using these sorts of terms, Virilio is not necessarily talking of the so-called 'postmodern city' of the postmodern urban geographers. He has, in fact, written about the city in conflict in the postwar period as more traditional urban geographers and urban sociologists have done. Los Angeles riots, conflicts in the French suburbs, riots in Handsworth, Toxteth, Brixton and Soweto have all come under Virilio's scrutiny. The difference between more standard approaches and that of Virilio is the technological input into the equation. He has seen with other commentators, including James Baldwin in the 1960s, that the urban disorder in cities the world over involves what he has referred to as a 'disqualification of an urban space once charged with meaning':

This urban Deregulation has effectively anticipated that of the new technologies: aeronautics, electronics, computers. Thanks to good old postindustrial restructuring, that sprawling urban wasteland where 'users' have contact only through the windshields of their cars is giving way at this very moment to the infinite suburb of an audiovisual no-man's-land peopled by ghosts, by electronic specters that hardly have any contact at all anymore except through the intermediary of a television screen or computer terminal, with their attendant voyeurism and all-out swapping – of sexual partners, shopping tips, sports scores, or purely denunciatory police intelli-gence. Audiovisual Gropes for which the annual information tech-nology trade fair does the publicity, perfectly reflecting a communications society that no longer communicates anything but Messages: data packets addressed to uncertain recipients – a data transfer accident that brings downtowns to the downfall James Baldwin decried some time ago. (Virilio 2000b: 72–3)

Writing or speaking in this vein, Virilio does come across as a conventional critic of late modernity, even at times injecting a moral-
ising or judgemental tone. On many matters of the city, violence
and its population changes, Virilio sounds like a sociologist from
the Chicago ecologist school of criminologists earlier in the
twentieth century, talking about disorganisation and breakdown
and twilight zones. He talks of our modern cities moving towards a
'solitary individuality', with the divorced couple and the single-
parent family, and people 'exchanging gestures but fewer and
fewer words'. This disorganisation of the cities for Virilio is nevertheless more the consequence of the acceleration of the reality of
time, or the acceleration of temporality, and its technological consequences, rather than conflict over housing, and the changes in
commercial centres of cities. 'Disintegration of community' and the
'catastrophic situation' in cities from Sao Paolo to Calcutta to
Washington to Paris is, for Virilio, brought about, or at least
exacerbated, by the 'absence' created by the connections to the
internet or to multimedia.

That is not to say that Virilio is not extremely useful in analysing
what some commentators have called 'postmodern culture'. The
speeding-up of culture, which includes the speeding-up of mass
communications, is in many ways the preferred jumping-off stage
to understand and appreciate such a culture. The effects of this in
Virilio's vista look rather different to postmodern media theorists'
interpretations. The 'disappearance' induced by speeded-up mass
communications in Virilio's vision of, for instance, the media
portrayal of a sporting event is curious. Speaking about the end of
the 1970s and the early 1980s, a point in history many theorists
take as the dawn of postmodern culture, Virilio saw that:

the serious problem is that those present, those who participate,
those for example who attend an auto race are disqualified by the
absentees. The billion people who watch the Olympic Games in
Moscow, or the soccer championship in Argentina, impose their
power at the expense of those present, who are already superfluous.
The latter are practically no more than bodies filling the stadium so
that it won't look empty. But their physical presence is completely
alienated by the absence of the television viewer. There's a
complete inversion, and that's what interests me in this situation.

Once the stadiums were full. It was a magnificent popular explosion. There were 200,000 people in the grandstands, singing and
shouting. It was a vision from ancient society, from the agora, from
paganism. Now when you watch the Olympics or the soccer
championship on television, you notice there aren't that many
people. And even they, in a certain way, aren't the ones who make
the World Cup. The ones who make the World Cup are the radios
and televisions that buy and – by favouring a billion and a half
television viewers – 'produce' the championship. Those absent
from the stadium are always right, economically and massively.
They have the power. The participants are always wrong. (Virilio
1997a: 87–8)

Even if in his later years television became less important to him,
in the 1970s Virilio clearly did watch a certain amount of television,
and his comments capture some of the 'feel' of televised live events
of the time such as the 1978 World Cup being played in Argentina
against the background of the multitude of 'disappeared' in that
country and the 1980 Olympic Games in Moscow boycotted on
political grounds by the USA. Virilio's discourse on televised sport
in the postmodern era is idiosyncratic, and it is an even more
accurate prediction of what was to happen over the subsequent
twenty years as pay TV and media moguls like Rupert Murdoch
and Silvio Berlusconi took their economic power to its limit. But on
any analysis of the 'postmodern' condition the work and thought
of Paul Virilio does not fall into the relevant criteria of the
categories usually used in these discussions. He does not hold to
any kind of relativist position, which is how postmodern politics is
often categorised. His Christianity has anchored him in a realist
position with regard to science and the human body. His position
on politics and justice is that of a 'democrat', as he has frequently
argued, and not comparable to the 'just gaming' of a postmodern
French theorist like his countryman Jean-François Lyotard.

In reality, Paul Virilio's work from the 1950s onwards has had
more in common with existentialist pyschology than 'post' theory
of any kind, be it post-structuralism, postmodernism or a disciplinary variant like 'postmodernist architecture'. The social theorist
Mike Gane (1993) has argued cogently that Jean Baudrillard's
development, whatever critics may say about him being guru of the

'post', can be seen to be rooted originally in Marcel Mauss' classic text *The Gift* and in theories of 'symbolic exchange'. Similarly, Virilio is best understood by tracing the actual influences on him over the years, as this book has done, rather than attributing false allegiances to him, however seemingly plausible in the first instance.

Paul Virilio has sometimes been bracketed with his more famous countryman and friend Jean Baudrillard as a 'postmodern philosopher'. The American neo-Marxist cultural theorist Douglas Kellner, for instance, refers to Virilio as a 'postmodern Jeremiah'. Others clearly brand Baudrillard with the same 'postmodernist' label, even when they are proclaiming the 'end of postmodernity'. In the case of both French theorists, Baudrillard and Virilio, however, it is quite possible to argue that they are best understood outside debates about postmodernity and postmodernism altogether. Jean Baudrillard has noted quite frankly that he is not a post-modernist. We are concerned here, of course, with Paul Virilio, not principally Jean Baudrillard, but equally it could be said, against some of the more idiosyncratic interpretations of Paul Virilio over the years, that Virilio, just as frankly, is not a postmodernist.

Critical modernism

Perhaps, given the application of the concepts of accelerated modernity and dangerous modernity used in this book to better understand and situate Virilio's wide-ranging thinking, it is more appropriate to concentrate on 'modernity'. Added to this, Paul Virilio has said explicitly in interview that 'postmodern' as a term 'never really appeared to me ... the modern is always the present'. Interestingly, also, Virilio has insisted on an 'instant present'. He is in many ways an 'historian of the present', although he might not always accept that label too readily, and, as we have seen, its relationship to the work of Foucault and governmentality makes it a confusing label in Virilio's case. In Virilio's universe it might be said to register, in mock-Situationist (circa 1968) slogan fashion, that 'Everything is Temporary in the Permanent Now'. Being for Virilio is 'being present here and now' where here has disappeared and there is only 'now'. The 'hyperconcentration of real time reduces all trajectories to nothing', in Virilio's view. According to

Paul Virilio, the 'temporal trajectory becomes a permanent present' as past, present and future are merged together and departure, voyage and arrrival become confused.

In this chapter we have introduced the idea of critical modernity to further locate Virilio's life and work beyond the concepts of accelerated modernity and dangerous modernity brought into play in previous chapters. In the case of critical modernity, however, it is a term that has been previously applied in relationship to Virilio. In the view of Claude Parent, Virilio's former architectural partner, a 'new modernity' or 'a critical modernity' was their most over-riding focus when he and Virilio were together as a working partnership in the 1960s, actively forging ahead of the contemporary thinking in architecture. Parent considered what they were doing was a 'cultural revolution' in architecture. The questions they were posing in the course of developing 'the function of the oblique' allowed them to 'consider anew the modern architecture of the 1920s and 1930s'. Virilio and Parent, both theoretically and practically, were trying to give a new critical inflection to modernist architecture in the 1960s. They were actively engaged in 'critical modernity'.

If 'critical modernity' might well be used as a general concept to explain Virilio's importance in the museum of critical theory, building on what we have described here as his contributions to an understanding of accelerated culture and dangerous modernity, it should, as with these other explanatory concepts, also be viewed with caution. Undoubtedly Paul Virilio, as we have seen, puts us on the way towards an explication of accelerated modernity through his notions of 'dromology', 'dromocracy', 'pure war' and the 'aesthetics of disappearance. He also sets us towards an understanding of dangerous modernity through 'the accident'. However, the realms of modernity described do not always necessarily fit with what Virilio has predicted. But it is to modernity, rather than tradition – or for that matter postmodernity – that Virilio's theoretical gaze on speed and technology looks. Where Karl Marx accurately captured modernity itself in the eternal phrase 'all that is solid melts into air', Virilio can be said to have penned its footnote with the 'aesthetics of disappearance'. Whilst Virilio has never been a Marxist, he is certainly a theorist of modernity in the wake of Marx. He is acutely aware that there is nothing *after* modernity apart from death. The death question is most important to Virilio, as a convinced Christian, although it engages him in a way that it never did the secular Marx. As Virilio has proclaimed it, unsurprisingly in view of what we have already noted about his theories of death, death has to do with speed, and also a redefinition of 'life':

> The question of death and the question of life are enormous philo-sophical problems. Life is generally identified with a biographical duration, a history – but a micro-history, that of an individual from birth to death. It's an historicistic view of life. Can we imagine life otherwise? Isn't life also a matter of intensity? That's the problem. Is the problem to live to be eighty, or is it to live until forty – but live intensely? ... I mean something you can experiment with. What does it mean to live a day intensely? I would say it's to put your finger on relativity. A day can last a thousand years and a thousand years can last a day. There's a relation of intensiveness that hasn't been politicised yet. Life has been linked to its duration, its slow development, its proliferation in generation, children, wealth, accumulation of inheritance, heirs, territory – in other words an extensive dimension. Can't we envision, isn't it incum-bent upon us to imagine, what an intensive life would be? Being alive means to be lively, quick. Being lively means being-speed, being-quickness. Being-liveliness. All these terms challenge us. There is a struggle, which I tried to bring to light, between metabolic speed, the speed of the living, and technological speed, the speed of death which already exists in cars, telephones, the media, missiles. (Virilio 1997a: 135–6)

Equally, Virilio believes that 'we must also stop fantasising about the effects of the genetics and biotechnological revolution', in other words the 'beyond humanity' condition, or in Francis Fukuyama's term 'posthumunanity', of robotics:

> A number of books talk about the surpassing of humans by artificial intelligence and medical care technology, as if Franken-stein was coming back. There is nothing beyond humanity. In this respect humanity is terminal, it is the end of God's miracles ... Humanity cannot be improved. There is no eugenics of the human race. (Virilio 1999: 88)

Virilio's religious beliefs do seem to hold him back on the third Einsteinian revolution, the population bomb, and particularly with regard to genetics and biotechnology. In 2002 Semiotext(e) published another book of interviews with long-time interlocutor Sylvère Lotringer, entitled *Crepuscular Dawn*, which includes a fascinating essay-cum-preface by Lotringer. The book ends with Virilio and Lotringer's reflections on 11 September 2001 in an eerie epilogue taped in May 2002 (which is where the book's contradictory title emerges). However, a large portion of the main interviews for the book (undertaken between November 1999 and May 2001) concentrates on 'the genetic bomb'. For Virilio, the genetic bomb marks a turn in the history of humanity. Artificial selection is, in his view, leading the way to a new eugenics. According to Virilio, this is the 'dawn' of a new racism, no longer 'endo-human' but 'trans-human' and 'exo-human'. For Virilio, the biological accident of science is a war against the human race. However, Virilio's religious-based beliefs certainly do not make him as reactionary as a figure like Francis Fukayama on the population, or genetic, bomb, issue. The more general question of what there is (if anything) after modernity is, of course, where Virilio's religious beliefs specifically complicate matters. Virilio has frequently said that he 'does not believe in death, but in the soul's immortality'. He does recognise however, that he, Paul Virilio, as a human being, is going to die and, although his favourite landscape is the coasts of Brittany, his actual chosen place of burial is apparently Normandy:

> Personally I was born in Paris but wouldn't want to be buried there. I'd rather be buried in Normandy, not far from the landing beaches where I walked around for a very long time. And if I had to choose the landscape of my death, it would be a small cemetery near Douvres-la-Déliverande in Calvados, halfway between the coast and the plains. (Virilio 1999: 112)

Life, then, leads to an end of sorts for Virilio. However, he knows, better perhaps than the multiple theorists of risk society, exactly what dangerousness in the society of the accident really means in terms of the risk to life. Just as we deemed it necessary to build on the concepts of accelerated modernity and dangerous modernity to demonstrate the value, and limits, of Virilio's thinking on speed, technology and the accident, so the idea of a new or critical modernity, or at least the 'possibility of and for critical thinking', demands that we look outside the narrowness of the term critical modernity as used by Claude Parent and Virilio in the context of the 1960s and architecture.

Modernity is still the starting-point. It is modernity as a concept that Virilio always returns to in his reflections on his writings in interviews. For Virilio the modern is 'now', 'not a past epoch – the fifteenth century, the beginning of the Renaissance or the end of the Middle Ages … I don't agree with any of that … the notion of modernity applies to the present'.

Just the two of us

It is the modern, rather than the postmodern condition, that interests Virilio. On the postmodern condition, perhaps more than anyone else, Virilio's countryman Jean-François Lyotard has mapped out the trajectory in terms of the collapse of grand narratives such as scientific progress. But Virilio does not buy the term. The 'postmodern' impulse in 'architecture', according to Virilio, has in any case 'virtually disappeared'. Postmodern theory has no place in Virilio's schema. In debates about the terms of what might make up postmodern theory (which in itself sounds to many like yet another grand, or meta, narrative), Virilio in particular has been over-shadowed by the academic and cultural superstardom of Jean Baudrillard and has been hampered by what has been a serious, and long-lasting, misinterpretation of the postmodern turn by academics all over the world and in various disciplines.

Both French theorists, Virilio and Baudrillard, have been heavily censured by critics for the lack of 'evidence' in their work as if they were social scientists. Baudrillard, at least, was once a sociologist but Virilio has never had such a post. Virilio has been criticised for eschewing 'primary evidence' and for not providing 'much in the way of secondary or supportive research to back his claims', much like the criticisms levelled at Jean Baudrillard by his more conservative critics.

Both writers have written about 'desertification' and have displayed a fascination with the 'desert' geographically and aesthetically.

Curiously, both writers have illustrated their written texts with their own personal photography. Baudrillard's interest in the photographer's art came later in life. The reissued *America* in the USA, for instance, today looks very different to the original text, published in France as *Amérique* in the 1980s, because it is profusely illustrated with Baudrillard's own photographs. Baudrillard has also published a large coffee-table book of his own photographs. Virilio has poked fun at Jean Baudrillard in interviews, drawing attention to his friend's relatively recent 'conversion' to a form which he had certainly not openly revered in the past. Virilio, of course, had pioneered photography as a 'research method' in his bunker archaeology work begun as long ago as the 1950s when 'architectural photographs' taken by Virilio himself were methodologically crucial to the work being done. Virilio has remembered that when he 'first met Baudrillard he had a real horror of images – a real horror'.

Significantly, some of the most important of Jean Baudrillard's controversial but innovative breakthroughs owe much, as he notes himself, to the less widely-read work of Paul Virilio. However, as we have seen, where Baudrillard sees 'trans-politics' as positive, Virilio sees it as 'totally negative'. As Virilio says in discussion with Sylvère Lotringer of Semiotext(e), 'I fight against the disappearance of politics'. In interview, Jean Baudrillard has been asked, 'What do you think of your own heirs. Paul Virilio, for example?' Baudrillard replied sympathetically:

> My heirs? Oh, Virilio is no heir. He's developed things in a very original manner. I find Virilio excellent, but he's more localised. At one and the same time he has simplified and radicalised the analysis of speed. I find all of that very, very strong. And in some sense it is more extreme, more extremist than my own analysis of the problem of speed and so on. But he is perhaps a little bit abstract. He is an analyst of a kind of catastrophe of time, of speed. But he remains an optimist of ... mmmm ... Well, he is a Christian! (laughter). This is not an argument, no ... But he is not an heir, as such, nor an associate in that sense. When I look around the French intellectual field there aren't many with whom I function with much affinity. There's Virilio, and then a few others who aren't known elsewhere. There is a great disparity among the theories. (Gane 1993: 41–2)

It might be tempting for critics to place Paul Virilio on the political spectrum somehow to the 'right' of someone like Jean Baudrillard who is regarded as on the ultra 'left' (that is, Virilio as a more 'conservative' version of Baudrillard) but it is instructive to see Baudrillard himself implying that Virilio's own analysis is very 'radical', even 'extreme'. Talk about the pot calling the kettle black! However, there is a serious point at stake here. Reading both of the two French theorists' contemporaneous tracts on the Gulf War of 1991, which it is possible to do in the original French and later English translations, it is actually the bleakness of Virilio's 'Desert Screen' theme which shines through. It is what Sean Cubitt, analysing and translating Virilio's Gulf War writing and comparing it with that of Baudrillard, describes, as we have seen already, in a particularly appropriate and rich phrase applied to Baudrillard and Virilio, as the 'poetics of pessimism'.

The two French theorists of the Gulf War did nevertheless differ considerably. For example, their views on the need to travel to the Gulf in order to write about the war certainly conflicted. Baudrillard commented at the time that he was not really interested in travelling to see the 'event' first-hand because he would not see anything, while in interview Virilio responded to Baudrillard's remarks with the phrase 'well, there we have different points of view'. Elsewhere, in interview, Baudrillard has been even more explicit about Virilio's moral stance, which he completely eschews:

> Others, even friends like Paul Virilio, take a position that is very clearly moral, in fact almost religiously so. His analysis of the contemporary situation is very radical, while on the other hand his judgement is much more moral. Ultimately, his analysis is more radical than mine, but in contrast to mine: I don't have any judgement like that. I know, for example, that he disagreed with what I said about the Gulf War not having taken place: 'The Gulf War is real, war is real'. It is this principle of reality that I think is the true moral principle. That's where we differ. (Baudrillard 2000: 139)

This is an extremely precise reflection by Baudrillard on the difference between the two theorists. Virilio does indeed rush to (ethical) judgement, something which Baudrillard avoids like the plague. Carlos Oliveira pointed out to Virilio in interview quite bluntly that 'your friend Baudrillard however simply negates the existence of reality in our society which has entered the realm of simulation'. Virilio definitely prefers the idea of virtual reality instead of Baudrillard's notion of simulation, a quite different way of conceptualising the history of the 'real'. Virilio told Oliveira in interview that one major difference between himself and Baudrillard was certainly over the question of 'reality' or, actually, 'realities':

> I disagree with my friend Baudrillard on the subject of simulation. To the word simulation, I prefer the one substitution. This is a real glass, this is no simulation. When I hold a virtual glass with a data glove, this is no simulation, but substitution. Here lies the big difference between Baudrillard and myself. I don't believe in simulationism, I believe that the world is already old-fashioned. As I see it, new technologies are substituting a virtual reality for an actual reality. And this is more than a phase: it's a definite change. We are entering a world where there won't be one but two realities, just like we have two eyes or hear bass and treble tones, just like we have stereoscopy and stereophony: there will be two realities: the actual and the virtual. Thus there is no simulation, but substitution. Reality has become symmetrical. The splitting of reality in two parts is a considerable event which goes far beyond simulation. (1995)

So virtual or substitution of reality rather than simulation is the bottom line for Virilio. The critical, or new modernity, which he has focused upon in the wake of the Second World War is finally brought out into the light in these comments on the fundamental gap between his ideas and those of Baudrillard, whose own trajectory as a long-time lapsed Marxist thinker has been the subject of so much (often misleading and wrong-headed) discussion itself in the international academy. For Virilio, their differences have always been clear and they stem partly from his own 'formal scientific education'. He has hinted that Baudrillard was lacking such a background education and that his friend was therefore at a disadvantage when he strayed into the realms of 'physics' and 'military sciences' when discussing 'reality'. He told Oliveira, again in crystal-clear language, in interview (originally in German):

> against the opinion of Baudrillard, I have to say that reality never vanishes. It constantly changes. Reality is the outcome of a pre-

determined epoch, science, or technique. Reality must be re-invented, always. To me, it is not the simulation of reality that makes the difference, it is the replacement of a pre-determined reality by another pre-determined reality. I proceed from the antagonism between real and virtual reality, and I notice that both will shortly constitute one single reality, but this will only take place through an unbelievable change that will have profound consequences for life; and these negative consequences are at the core of my writing. (1995)

The differences between Virilio and Baudrillard may lie less in a question of 'formal scientific education' than in the long-standing influence of Gestalt pyschology and the phenomenology of perception of Paul Virilio, on the one hand, and, on the other hand, the more 'literary' 'poetics' background of the 'forgotten' 1960s Baudrillard before he became an international academic superstar. Whatever the origins of their difference, different on this crucial issue of the 'reality' of modernity they most certainly are. This, too, is what makes Virilio's vision possibly even bleaker than that of Baudrillard, who thinks that in 'the perfect crime' we have managed to kill off reality. Virilio, in opposition to Baudrillard, has said, again in interview with Carlos Oliveira:

> We face a duplication of reality. The virtual reality and the 'real' reality double the relationship to the real, something that to the best of my knowledge, results in clear pathological consequences .. 'To be' used to mean to be somewhere, to be situated, in the here and now, but the 'situation' of the essence of being is undermined by the instantaneity, the immediacy and the ubiquity which are characteristic of our epoch. Our contemporaries will henceforth need two watches: one to watch the time, the other to watch the place where one actually is. This double-watch will be necessary for the duplication of reality that is occurring. Reality is becoming a stereo-reality. (1995)

Virilio, too, has pointed to another difference between Jean Baudrillard and himself: that of the question of death. Virilio has put the difference succinctly:

> Death isn't sad, it's Being itself. Death is the founder of consciousness, and therefore of political awareness ... All I want to say is simply that political inquiry into death doesn't exist. Even when

> I read Jean Baudrillard's book *L'Echange Symbolique et la Mort* (Symbolic Exchange and Death) – I'm sorry, but there's not a single warrior in it! (Virilio 1997a: 122)

He may not be a fan of Baudrillard's key text on symbolic exchange and death but Virilio does share with his friend the impact of what he calls 'primitive societies' (and their symbolic exchange) on his thinking, especially in the context of death. Virilio said about his childhood amongst the Breton peasants during the Second World War:

> primitive societies ... place death at their centres. And from this point of view I feel closer to rural societies than my contemporaries. Primitives are at the heart of questions about death, science, politics and war ... I spent my youth in Breton peasant families where, even though they were Christians, every evening around the fire we discussed myths, great pagan tales, the cart-driver of death: death is a cart that you hear coming, which carries you off. (Virilio 1997a: 130)

The liberal condition

We have a sense, after the previous discussion, of Virilio – and perhaps of Baudrillard too – as primarily a theorist of the modern condition. But the modern condition is changing. As we have made clear in this present book, Virilio's work has sometimes been seen by critics and commentators to be an instructive and incisive analysis of themes such as the cinematic gaze, the collapse of time and space, speed and war, and politics of the urban condition in what the postmodern theorist Jean-François Lyotard, in the 1970s, saw as the 'postmodern condition'. It has also been seen by critics and commentators as a resource for rebuilding the 'social' and the 'political' domains of global culture. So what kind of modernity are we talking about here? For Virilio it may not be postmodern but it is certainly fragmented and cut-up. Virilio has spoken of Jean-François Lyotard approvingly, especially in the context of what Lyotard calls, in *The Postmodern Condition*, a text originally produced as a report on science, the 'disappearance of the great narratives'. Virilio told Sylvère Lotringer in the early 1980s shortly after Lyotard's book had become internationally influential:

There is only collage, cutting and splicing. This explains fairly well what Jean-François Lyotard calls the disappearance of the great narratives. Classless society, social justice – no one believes in them any more. We're in the age of micro-narratives, the art of the fragment ... History is on the level of the great narrative. I only believe in the collage: it's trans-historical. (Virilio 1997a: 41)

Fragmented or not, the focus for Virilio, however, has always been 'modernity', or the 'modern condition' of critical modernity, and he brings a critical perspective to it, especially on technology. However flawed this perspective, it is distinct from other cultural and political theorists, including Jean Baudrillard. It is this modern condition of critical modernity that Virilio uncovers and illumin- ates in an idiosyncratic way. The 'return to politics', which he says his work prefigures, is a politics about the precise nature of this modernity. But whether what he says contributes to other crucial questions of modernity such as the nature and history of liberal governmentality is much more dubious.

Unlike Michel Foucault, Virilio does not see it as his task to con- struct a history of liberalism and governmentality. Virilio's Catholic anti-statism is a huge obstacle in this regard too, and he never overcomes such a handicap. Politically, Virilio is in most senses of the word a liberal, high modernist, rather than a postmodernist thinker. Sean Cubitt (Cubitt 1999) has argued that 'Virilio's position is liberal-humanist', with the liberalism stemming from 'a belief that we inhabit a militarised society on a trajectory towards the classical liberal scenario of apocalypse' and the humanism emanating 'from a Christian phenomenology'. We do not have to agree with Cubitt that we should really stand Virilio theoretically 'on his head' (as Marx did to Hegel) if 'we are to make any use' of him to recognise the accuracy of the general sketch of Virilio's position. Virilio's intellectual tradition is accurately characterised as one which consistently throughout his adult life has embraced phenomenology and liberal, even religious, humanism. This position is in sharp contrast to Baudrillard on the one hand, and the nihilism and rela- tivism of some of the burgeoning postmodernist theorists around the globe on the other. Unlike the 'New Philosophers' (*Nouveaux Philosophes*) of the 1970s in France, with whom he is sometimes lumped by careless critics, Virilio was never a Marxist and therefore had nothing to renounce in the way of a particular brand of Trotskyism, Leninism, Maoism or Stalinism. He has, however, described André Glucksmann, one of the leading *Nouveaux Philosophes*, as a fellow intellectual of defence and a 'war baby' like himself. Virilio's Christianity, as we have seen in this book, has been an ever-present influence in his life and work since 1950. Among other effects of his religious faith is his claim to be a 'pacifist', which has, in Virilio's own reflection, 'meaning (which I adopt) insofar as it is linked to faith ... You know that I'm a Christian, and as a Christian I reject nuclear faith because I believe in the peace of Christ.' As a committed Christian since the age of eighteen, Virilio did not therefore suddenly convert to Catholicism in the mid 1970s. He generally escaped vilification at the time, unlike other contemporaries, such as the French 'New' Philosophers, who were subjected to rejection and criticism by the international left in the 1970s.

Furthermore, to conflate Virilio's long trajectory with some kind of anarchistic or ultra-leftist 'techno-politics', as some commentators have done (Armitage 2000c, 2000b, 2000a), is as misleading as it was to call him a Situationist or anarchist in May 1968. Some critics (Kellner 1998), who try in vain to assess Virilio's theoretical work in the context of such a project of 'techno-politics' or even 'accelerated aesthetics', end up making him out to be something of a 'reactionary', which he certainly is not; others make him out to be more of a leftist romantic than he actually has ever been, while continually criticising his supposed 'premodern' stances on modernity and postmodernity. Virilio has written and talked a good deal about democracy in dromocracy. He has been clear and unequivocal as a straightforward centrist or left-liberal humanist:

> I am, of course, a democrat. I always have been, yet in my opinion there is no power without laws or regulations. Regulation of a book, of a constitution, and thus of a justice. There is a justice of wealth and economy, thus one of distribution. There is also an economy and a justice of speed. In the past the nobility was originally a class of speed just like the cavalry. All the hick had was his cows! The question of speed is actually that of democratisation ... multimedia confronts us with a question: will we be able to achieve a democracy of real time, LIVE time, a democracy of immediacy and ubiquity. (Virilio 1999: 16–17)

For Virilio, living in a society with absolute speed has come an 'almost divine power' which questions the possibility of democracy. He fears that because 'we have achieved the three attributes of the divine: ubiquity, instantaneity, immediacy', this is no longer 'a question of democracy' but 'tyranny'. Virilio has seen the political problem acutely, as he revealed in an interveiw with Philippe Petit:

> The tyranny of real time is not very different from classical tyranny, because it tends to destroy the reflection of the citizen in favour of a reflex action. Democracy is based on solidarity, not solitude, and man has to reflect before acting. Now, real time and the world present demand a reflex from the television viewer that is really a kind of manipulation. The tyranny of real time is tantamount to a subjugation of the television viewer. The temporality of democracy is threatened, because the expectation of a judgement tends to be eliminated. Democracy is the expectation of a decision made collectively. LIVE democracy, or automatic democracy, eliminates this reflection and replaces it with a reflex. Ratings replace elections, and the microchip card replaces deliberation. This is extremely dangerous for democracy in terms of the decision and voting time. Ratings and polls become electoral. The poll is the election of tomorrow, virtual democracy for a virtual city. (Virilio 1999: 87)

This interview statement is in many ways a fairly standard liberal democratic position on democracy and electoral politics. Virilio does not much deviate from it in his writings or in his political actions. He has exclaimed 'personally I am not a militant. I could not be one. I can only watch and wait.' His praxis certainly differs a great deal from the views of a theorist like Michel Foucault on democracy and justice. Foucault's neo-Maoist positions on popular justice in the 1970s were never shared by Virilio, despite his flirtations with the ideas of the Italian Autonomists. Virilio also sees the judges and the legal system as implicated in this impending tyranny of the media:

> I think the political parties are both threatened and threatening. Judicial revolt, the republic of judges, could only have happened because of the existence of a media class. If you can't understand the role of television inside the civil courts in the United States or

Italy, then you can't understand the emergence of the legal class. What is disturbing is not that the judges are doing their job, but rather that they had to climb on the shoulders of the media class in order to get rid of the political class. It is disturbing that they were duped and that they took advantage of the threat represented by the media class to the political class in order to get out of a bad situation ... With the O. J. Simpson trial, we saw what a Live trial could be under the eyes of the cameras. The jurors were lynched, and under pressure from the media, they could not make a free verdict. (Virilio 1999: 93–4)

As we have already seen, Virilio does not share the Foucauldian view on people's justice or on the need to radicalise punishment and law and the state. Virilio's views on political democracy and justice systems also differ considerably from someone like Jean Baudrillard. He has encapsulated the explicit political difference in interview with Sylvère Lotringer:

Trans-politics is the beginning of the disappearance of politics in the dwindling of the last commodity: duration. Democracy, consultation, the basis of politics requires time. Duration is the proper of man; he is inscribed within it. For me, trans-politics is the beginning of the end. That's where my understanding of it radically differs from Jean Baudrillard's; for him it's positive. For me it's totally negative. I fight against the disappearance of politics. I'm not saying that we should revert to ancient democracy, stop the clock and all that. I'm saying that there's work to be done ... in order to re-establish politics, at a time when technology no longer portions out matter and geographical space (as was the case in ancient democratic society) but when technology portions out time – and I would say: the depletion of time. (Virilio 1997a: 34)

As we have discussed already, like Baudrillard, Virilio is in many ways an anti-postmodernist, although they differ on the nature of what modernity itself is and what can be done about it. Mike Gane has made a good case for seeing Baudrillard as an anti-postmodernist and it is possible to argue the same kind of position for Paul Virilio too. We have emphasised in this book that what marks out a terrain of difference between them is Virilio's struggle with a critical modernity. Gane has gone as far as to emphasise what he sees as Baudrillard's 'anti-modernist' position. The same could not be said of Virilio, who maintains a critical engagement with modernity, and in this regard he is also distinct from someone like the theorist of science Bruno Latour (who has claimed that 'we never were modern') with whom he has occasionally been linked (Crawford 2000). Virilio is often lambasted for his 'Catholic faith' and its drawbacks for his theoretical framework. He has, in many ways, been at the same time a proud, often moderate, liberal-humanist, critical thinker in what, as he has got older, is undoubtedly an age of neo-conservativism, barren of much critical modernist political thought. Paul Virilio predates, and in some ways displaces, the post-structuralism of Louis Althusser, Michel Foucault and Jacques Lacan, and the deconstruction of Jacques Derrida, but he shares their scepticism of the Enlightenment tradition. Neither, however, is he squarely in the opposition Habermas camp on modernity (Brigham 1996): Jurgen Habermas' definition of the Enlightenment tradition is 'too narrow' in Virilio's eyes. But an alternative perspective, of the 'rival enlightenments' emerging out of conflicts about modernity and the construction of a secular state in seventeenth-century Europe, would find Virilio's Catholic anti-statism placing him in a particular Enlightenment tradition which would be less liberal than that of Habermas.

Virilio's prominent liberal intellectual stance over the years has meant that he is able with some authority to warn against the possibilities of totalitarianism in the global culture of the millennium. He has, as we have seen, described the twentieth century as 'hyperviolence'. But Virilio also perceives the potential of virtual reality and the enormous implications of what he sees as the communications revolution now taking place, where 'time' not 'place' is of the essence. Indeed, Claude Parent has argued that tuning in to the times has always been Virilio's special skill, whether it be the Situationism of May 1968, the threat of global 'terrorism' of the 1990s, or the 'posthumanity' of the twenty-first century. Parent has summed up his former younger partner with a brutally honest backward glance:

> Virilio has always had a talent for tuning in to current trends and events and interpreting them in his own distinctive way to give them a new dimension. That, I believe, is the basis of his approach.
> (Virilio and Parent 1996: 55)

The personal is the personal

Claude Parent is correct to point to the fact that Virilio is magpie-like in his method of absorbing other thinkers and their thought. However, one trend Virilio has never seemed to latch onto in any substantial way is feminism. John Armitage has noted quite pointedly that Virilio 'does not appear to be acquainted with feminist inspired accounts of technology and subjectivity like those provided by Donna Haraway', although Virilio himself has let it be heard that he has personally known French feminist and literary theorist Luce Irigaray for many years. He has also expressed an 'interest' in feminism to Sylvère Lotringer in interviews conducted in the 1980s. Virilio claimed, however, that feminism is 'shot':

> I am quite interested in women's liberation. Luce Irigaray is a very old friend of mine and I like the research she's doing into female identity very much: it's the will to manifest an identity which would not be known, which would be revealed in its absolute originality. It's a mad and passionate experiment, which to my mind, resembles the invention of dietary customs. We must have begun like that. Culture came out of a similar will to create difference. Aside from this marvellous invention which I support entirely, the political dimension of the women's liberation movement is shot, as far as I can tell. Because they don't take into account the geo-political dimension, the situation of Pure War, of absolute deterrence. (Virilio 1997a: 111–2)

Virilio has occasionally been asked about sexual identity and 'domestic economy' in interviews but there has been relatively little general comment on Paul Virilio and feminism in any of the literature on, or interviews with, him, apart from an essay by Verena Andermatt Conley in *Theory, Culture and Society*, edited by John Armitage. There are very few references indeed in Virilio's eclectic citations to any female writers in his hundreds of translated or untranslated writings. One characteristic of Virilio's work is that the written work frequently feels as if it exists in something of a time warp. His essays and books seem untouched by the fierce battles over sexuality that have torn through Western academia and elsewhere during the period that Virilio has held his academic post as a Professor of Architecture: that is, the late 1960s, 1970s,

1980s and 1990s. Queer theory and feminism do not appear to register in his writings in any way.

It is certainly in the area of sexuality too, where Virilio often seems less than sure-footed (Virilio 1981). For instance, he has explained part of his dromology by reference to the 'vehicle' (Virilio 1989a), and he seems regularly to identify the 'first' vehicle in his writing with the figure of 'woman'. When he has ever drawn on social background, he has conceived of heterosexuality as a male and female couple where the woman is 'mounted' by the man, a sexual and social situation where the woman 'carries' the man. For Virilio, furthermore, the heterosexual couple forms the primitive 'war machine'! In what actually sounds like a rare effort by an interviewer to probe the personal life of Paul Virilio, Philippe Petit, in one of the wide-ranging discussions conducted in the mid 1990s for the book *Politics of the Very Worst*, asked him the direct question: 'What do sex and love mean for you?' Virilio completely ignored the personal implications of the issue and noted that the 'loss' of sex has increasingly meant 'cybersex', which itself is 'disappearing' and being replaced by 'fear':

> Fear of the other is the very opposite of love. It's easy to forget that when one thinks of love in terms of eroticism, sexuality and the pleasures of the flesh. The question of love is the opposite of hate, or the fear of others. Hatred is born out of fear. Today we are witnessing a disintegration of the populating unit. For the people of the city, the populating unit represents the family and the populating site represents the city ... today, in the metacity – or the virtual city – we have the single parent family. The family line no longer exists, the family disintegrates. The woman or the man leaves with the children. We have therefore reached the end of a cycle, or the beginning of a reciprocal exclusion. Divorce is not merely a phenomenon of mores, but a phenomenon of the human race, and teletechnologies highlight this. Telesexuality (or cyber-sexuality) comes on top of events that were already cataclysmic. (Virilio 1999: 61–2)

In answer to further questioning by Philippe Petit, Virilio admitted – perhaps repairing past gaps in his reading schedule – that he had 'found a text' on 'cyberfeminism' in the journal *Chimère* organised by his friend Félix Guattari, and noted (in these mid 1990s conversations) that 'cyberfeminism has existed in the United States for a while now'. Not surprisingly, distance ('long-distance work', 'long-distance love'), or at least the melting-away of distance, seems to have preoccupied Virilio's thinking on the future of love and sex:

> with video-pornography, for example, this distance is at its height. And with the pink Minitel, there is only a voice – the Minitel is used for more than just making dates – there's the telephone for that. Now, we have cybersex and telesexuality in which divorce is at its height because we are splitting up. It is no longer a couple divorcing, but rather a divorce of copulation! (Virilio 1999: 62)

Minitel is the French internet service which reaches many millions of people in France but it is less the specific technology which takes up Virilio's interest than the effects of 'telesexuality':

> this has nothing to do with any kind of morality, but is instead related to demography, let me take an example: Flaubert's or Maupassant's prostitute ... is a woman that you are friends with. In today's cities, the prostitute is the girl in the shop window! It's very much a product. If you consider the striptease or the peepshow, there is no fear of the other, but a retreat or distancing. (Virilio 1997a: 62)

This condition is the end of a cycle of 'sexual alterity' for Virilio. However, time is once again of the essence for him when it comes to modern sexuality, and what he has elsewhere referred to in his approaches to various factors and features of modernity as a 'rhythmology' is possible when it comes to an analysis of contemporary sexuality and society. He has argued that:

> As for divorce, I think there is a problem of temporality. Consider the way people lived in the last century. The life that a couple led was completely different from that of a contemporary couple. The pressure of the city, the rapidity of exchanges, the stress and acceleration of mores all contribute to the fact that in five years, a modern couple has lived the equivalent of fifty years of a couple in the nineteenth century. So having lived fifty years in five years, they can no longer stand to live together ... These are phenomena of 'tempo'. There is a rhythmology to public life. People can get along at a certain rhythm, but if this rhythm is accelerated, they snap. (Virilio 1999: 64)

The personal, then, is a domain to which Paul Virilio has had trouble accommodating. In reality, relatively little is known in the international academy about Virilio's own personal life and the impact it may have had on the work he has done since the 1950s. He is seldom portrayed in photographs beyond the occasional head shot, although there are now widely-available photographs of Virilio with Parent in the 1960s and of Virilio photographing bunkers in the late 1950s. James Der Derian (Der Derian 1998), who has helped to furnish Virilio watchers with new translations, has described him, after meeting him to record an interview, as 'short, broad-chested, strong-featured and somewhat pugnacious in manner' and 'not terribly open about himself'. Der Derian, an academic from the USA, has also said that he thought of Paul Virilio as 'a kind of Norman Mailer who prefers red wine to bourbon'!

There is no sustained effort in Virilio's writings to stray far from the war, technology and speed focus which has sustained his interest for so long. Generally, these kinds of subjects have been written about mainly by men, and they are often described as 'boys' toys'. This label refers both to the high-technology weapons of war, and the chronicling of the speed of its change. Curiously too, those on the liberal-left of politics, where Virilio certainly is positioned, have not written much about such topics. It has been left to right-wing or neo-conservative critics in the main to write about war and technological speed. Generally, in Virilio's case, the personal has remained the personal. He does not like to use himself as an example in his writing so we learn little about him. Nevertheless, from Virilio's perspective, the personal is disappearing and the excessive tempo of the modern city is creating a loss which can only be resolved by:

> taking back language. Here again we find the words of Aesop. Language is the worst of things and the best of things. This paradox is at the heart of the information revolution. Taking back language means talking with one another. Media information prevents us from doing this, and this is quite evident in the suburbs. Why is there violence? Because we no longer talk to one another ... In order to take back language, we have to abandon certain types of activities. I don't want to use myself as an example, because I believe there are many others, but now I don't have a car or a fax

machine, I don't watch television anymore, and I rarely listen to the radio; which means I'm reading again. When you deny yourself reading and writing, you deny yourself language and thus, contact with others. Socialisation occurs with languages. The best way to love one another is through language. This social necessity is largely threatened by the information technologies. (Virilio 1999: 64)

Paul Virilio in this kind of mode, or mood, is quite mournful, even nostalgic. It is easy to see why, despite his long-term claim to be a lover of the new technologies, he is sometimes regarded with scepticism by interviewers and reviewers who regularly cite him as a 'prophet of doom' or 'apocalyptic' in his pronouncements and thinking. Perhaps it is more a question of fatigue. Virilio has more recently felt a weight of responsibility in the lifelong task he has chosen to undertake. He has referred with sadness to the 'loss' not only of sociality in the cities but the personal loss through death of influential Frenchmen such as the theologian Jacques Ellul and the theorist Gilles Deleuze, who, Virilio has noted, 'was also interested in technology through the desiring machines'. For Paul Virilio, his work in an increasingly lone-ranger role as analyst of technology – in an age when 'we have lost some degree of assurance' and we have trouble reorienting ourselves – is actually 'becoming super-human'.

CHAPTER FIVE

Forget Virilio

As we mentioned earlier in this book, there are many reasons to remember Paul Virilio, both in terms of the uncollected or hidden Virilio of the 1950s and 1960s that we excavated in Chapter 1 and the many insights which we have covered in other pages of this book. The architectural work he conducted with Claude Parent in the 1960s, both theoretical and practical, is especially worth remembering. But throughout the book we have also pointed to the numerous problems with Virilio's work, then and now. This chapter makes an assessment of these elusive points 'for and against' Virilio. The ultimate conclusion is that having remembered Virilio for all kinds of reasons and set him properly in context, taking into account all that he has actually written and said in French and in translation, not to mention what others have said about him, we should perhaps consider forgetting Virilio. He is a significant contemporary thinker certainly but contemporary cultural thinking of the twenty-first century will need other resources too, if we are to keep up with the rapidity of change (which, of course, Virilio has taught us about) and the persistence of tradition in modernity.

So, we have reached the end. The end of *a* book if not the 'end of the book'. Virilio does not believe in the end of the book as some of his contemporaries have envisioned it. Jean-François Lyotard, in the preface to his book *The Differend*, written in the last century, opined that 'in the next century there will be no more books' because it 'takes too long to read when success comes from gaining time'. The end of duration is upon us and post-literate culture will have its day, in other words. This is a very 'Virilian' scenario in many ways if we take seriously some of the more extreme statements he has made, but Paul Virilio's actual solution is a rather old-fashioned one: to write short, rapid works which overlap with each other. Many of his interview conversations are everyday explanations of the same ideas that are slightly more embroidered in the short books. He certainly does not believe in producing voluminous works. The Semiotext(e) 'little black book' series seemed tailor-made for Virilio: little 'logic bombs' that could be stored away in the back pocket, dropped on us from a great height when all around us seemed chaotic and in a state of flux, even if we did not seem to be moving very fast at the time.

The final end

Nevertheless, the 'final chapter' of a book is always significant, especially a final chapter of a book on Paul Virilio. Virilio himself has proudly stated:

> The last chapters of my books are always important because in the final account I don't believe in writing several books. You could publish them in an enormous dictionary in which everything would come chronologically. (Virilio 1997a: 46)

Reading thoroughly what Virilio has actually written and said, rather than what a cursory reading of a couple of unconnected texts might suggest, produces surprising conclusions. Virilio might well be criticised for not really saying that much when all his works are put together chronologically, a practice he has himself suggested. There is an extensive overlap of ideas. He has admitted that one book often represents the development and completion of another one, 'all of this is echoed' in each book, and that together the books all 'form a whole'. The 'end of the book' in Virilio's work actually never comes. Perhaps we should, as already intimated, just forget Virilio? Even before the final interruption, or death, comes for him, as it comes to us all, and we are forced to look back on the end of the author Paul Virilio (1998b).

Forgetting Virilio is not necessarily an easy task. To be sure, his scattergun writing style is not always easy to follow, often provoking disorientation and dislocation at the very least. Insights, personal memories, detailed histories, major theoretical leaps and banalities sit side by side. Indeed, some readers respond to the English translations of his work with exasperation: for instance, the pop-culture theorist Simon Reynolds, whilst acknowledging a theoretical debt to fellow French theorists Gilles Deleuze and Félix Guattari, who have certain things in common with Paul Virilio (Crogan, 2000), has exclaimed after reading Virilio, 'Why can't he put his thoughts logically together?' Deleuze and Guattari themselves are not known for the clarity and ease of accessibility of their writings and for Virilio to be described as less logical than the theorists of Nomadology is somewhat damning. Some reviewers have even resorted to describing Virilio's work as 'slightly mad' after reading him. The aphoristic style of Virilio, in books, articles and interviews – although nowhere near as extreme in this regard as that of his friend Jean Baudrillard – is clearly disconcerting for an English-speaking audience and some of the translations from the French, in the early years at least, have not helped the potential readership to adapt. Reading Virilio thoroughly does leave the reader with the feeling of many dislocated, undeveloped ideas swirling around, often at a level of great generality. The content is often not particularly logical if viewed from a conventional academic perspective in the human or social sciences. Some issues on which Virilio has provoked the critics are stylistic. The italicisation of words and phrases which peppers Virilio's work looks quite different on the page in the 'cool' 'Collection L'Espace Critique' series which he created for Galilée, compared to the frequently bold lettering of the same words and phrases in the English translations. 'Cryptic' too is a word we might reserve for Virilio's writings and not merely for his interpretation of architecture in the 1950s and 1960s. One of my colleagues, on reading an early draft of a chapter of this present book, commented 'very pithy' (at least I think that is what she said!), as if the book's style was unconsciously or subconsciously imitating the mode of many of the outpourings of its ultimate subject, and object, Paul Virilio.

Unlike most academic writers, Virilio has specialised in writing short books. He has praised Sun Tsu's *The Art of War*, which, as he notes, is 'only 120 pages long' contrasting it with the tomes of that other military guru Clausewitz. As we have seen, Virilio praised his own little book *Speed and Politics* as 'a rapid book' but 'a key book'. He seems pleased to be able to say about his work in general that he never writes 'long things'. Certainly, in Virilio's writings little space is ever wasted. They are worthy of re-reading and are at the very least thought-provoking and 'suggestive' (a description he himself favours) of further reading and study, which is how Paul Virilio, self-reflexively, has always characterised his enterprise. As Claude Parent said about him in the 1960s, he is a wide-ranging reader. The range of his sources (often completely unconnected and mystifying) is always impressive, and in particular the use he makes of contemporary military and other official sources can be imitated by researchers today interested in writing about the important issues related to the so-called revolutions in military affairs and the security services, especially in the USA. Lastly, Paul Virilio is probably one of the easiest of French theorists to absorb, although for some readers that may not be saying very much.

Pop goes Virilio

Low culture is not something with which Virilio has ever dirtied his hands. He is in the main a 'serious' theorist and also a 'surfer' of academic, high or serious culture. Unlike Jean Baudrillard, the banality of low or popular culture is seldom in his sights and the jokeyness, mischievousness even, of Baudrillard rarely seems evident. But Paul Virilio's writings have long had a major role in the theoretical socio-legal studies sub-discipline of 'law and popular culture' which has operated at the intersection of critical legal studies and cultural studies for over two decades. When work in this sub-discipline was first done on accelerated youth culture, as it was in the mid and late 1980s, it certainly did try to adapt some of the 'pithiness' of the small number of the Semiotext(e) 'Virilios' then available in Manchester, England, for the apparently alien purpose of explaining and archiving the 'end-of-the-century party' and the 'hedonism in hard times' which were sweeping the green and unpleasant land ruled by neo-liberalism and the governments of Margaret Thatcher. These popular cultural formations like 'acid house' and 'rave culture', and their rapid successors, were very shortly afterwards to be found across the globe in the 1990s. Whether these attempts at experimental 'history of the present' failed or not, Virilio's shadowy presence was always there within and without the writing. The accelerated culture which academic colleagues were attempting to capture meant that 'subcultures' or 'cults' which had taken years in the past to come to the attention of the media were now more likely to exist only for days (if that) before they were devoured by media culture. The time between some phenomenon being underground, then overground (and then underground again) seemed almost nil. 'Pop time' as it was originally described and reformulated, appeared at the time very much like the 'instant present' of parallel velocities (Peters 2000), where everything moves at the speed of life (Luke 1998). Meanwhile, Paul Virilio was predicting such accelerated temporality for more general cultural and technological change at the end of the century.

To some extent, to use the writing of Virilio for a theoretical and contemporary historical analysis of youth and popular culture was self-consciously a contradiction in terms. Theorists in other cultures and countries (Wark 1988) have not imported Virilio in order to theorise the popular or the low cultural fields. This is not surprising. Virilio's own examples of 'culture' are rarely from a domain which could be labelled 'popular' (when he cites references they are virtually always high or avant-garde culture), and he has hardly ever shown any sophisticated knowledge of youth culture. He has really only noted it in the context of attacks on 'time', on the race against the historical clock. For instance, he has connected it with post-'May '68' culture:

> After the *artistes maudits* of the nineteenth century came the lost generations of the so-called roaring twenties. With them we were to see a democratisation of the trend. We went from Scott Fitzgerald to Kerouac and a Beat generation with suicidal and criminal tendencies; then came the angelism of Woodstock and the final upsurge of 1968 where, as Hannah Arendt foresaw, imagination would not come to power. After them would come the enforced idleness of the new losers and the various other junkies, the swelling ranks of the social dregs of a post-industrial world. The dreams of liberation of a formerly oppressed youth, avid for change, have in fact always led to dictatorships and repressive paramilitary systems. After Hitler and Stalin of the Soviet Union – even though after the First World War that country was seen as the Mecca of this youthful cultural revolution – we come to the new technological nannying offered to the world by the American nation which has plunged into a complete globalitarian frenzy. And we do so merely because the adverts for its old traditional products (Coke, jeans, Hollywood, Mickey Mouse etc) paradoxically present the image of a young country. Young or, more accurately, Infantile. (Virilio 2000c: 99)

The 'infantilisation' of international youth culture at the end of the century is a book-length subject in itself but Virilio's intervention does not take us very far. In a sense, the question might be why should he have any great knowledge of, or expertise on, postwar youth culture? His own youthful experience, as we have seen throughout this book, was materially shaped by the Second World War and a strong religious faith. War was his university and he agreed with Sylvère Lotringer in interview that he had never stopped being a 'student' of the Second World War, an event which, for Virilio at least, has never ended, legally or culturally. Virilio's life was not touched very much by postwar pop culture. Nicholas Zurbrugg interrogated him, in interview, on precisely this kind of potential gap in his writing and his teaching, asking Virilio whether he felt in the mid 1990s, 'a certain sense of frustration when confronted by a younger generation that knows nothing of this experience and that judges contemporary culture on the basis of its publicity and its pop culture?' Virilio made the salient and honest reply that 'yes, that happens with my students', but that even though he had 'many students who know nothing about Hitler', he had 'many Lebanese refugee students – also many Pakistani, Israeli, Syrian and Iraqi and Iranian students' at his classes in Paris. In one of the rare insights we get into Virilio's teaching over his thirty years in the academy, he remembered that 'during the recent wars in these regions, many students came to study' with him because they found that, with Virilio as their professor, they 'could talk about the war'. His indigenous French students were apparently 'astonished by all this, because they knew nothing about it'. 'Sometimes', Virilio recalled, 'I'd suggest that students should take planes to Beirut – and some of them went to Beirut during the war and came back transfigured.' 'War studies' had been a subject of long-standing interest to Virilio the university academic and teacher, even if it had no formal place on the curriculum.

Nevertheless, despite not alighting on the subject very often, Paul Virilio did speak about youth culture very cryptically in the 1997 *Pure War* 'afterword' interview with Sylvère Lotringer, leaving the interesting follow-up questions tantalisingly closed-off. Lotringer pushed him on the important issue of 'real space' having been replaced by 'real time', and Virilio used youth culture as an example:

> Real time reigns supreme. That's why music is the art of reference, that is an art of time and acceleration. It's an art of time and speed. It's even the first to have given form to speed. It's not by chance that young people only have one art, and that's music. It carries the

rest of them with it. It's extraordinary that the only thing that stands in the way of television is music. (Virilio 1997a: 172)

Virilio and Lotringer agreed in this conversation that 'music is more and more linked to technology', and that (at least when he spoke about it in the mid 1990s) the 'hottest music to date is techno, industrial, synthesising etc'. Virilio has said elsewhere that 'music and speed are inseparable'. He is again sufficiently on the ball to realise that 'techno' and associated forms of 1990s dance culture were clearly good instances of this to cite in support of his general thesis on speed and culture. To Virilio, 'dance is an extraordinary thing, more extraordinary than most people usually think' and the notion is clearly important to him. Dance 'preceded writing, speaking and music', he has controversially stated. He has developed these ideas in interviews and essays that explore what he calls the 'traces of dance'. Furthermore, Virilio has strongly supported the idea that the problem of technology generally is 'a question of rhythm' which is 'one of the great questions today'. It is for that reason that he is always, he says, 'interested in the proximity between speed and music'. Acknowledging that we have a 'rhythmology for music – the whole history of instrumental music', he also contends that he likes 'dance, because, apart from musical rhythm, there's no mediation, there's just the body'. Certainly BPM, or beats per minute (135, 165, 210 or whatever), had become increasingly significant in electronic dance music during the 1990s and styles like 'gabba', 'hardcore' or 'nosebleed' took the music of global youth culture to new, body-disturbing speeds. Virilio could have written extensively about this if he had had sufficient knowledge of the area. In the 1990s Virilio's speed theory really had found its time, although he did not personally overtly recognise, or exploit, it to any great degree.

Curiously, Virilio has not shown much sense of his contemporary relevance in this sphere. There are, however, 'traces' or 'tracks' of Virilio all over the place. For instance *Velocity* is actually the title of a US-based dance magazine which looks at accelerated popular culture. But Virilio does not appear to know about such examples. He has left it to others to apply his provocative 'suggestions' and 'implicit' readings in contemporary popular cultural debate. He has seemed to be content in interviews to utter one-word answers like 'techno' when asked about music and speed but, importantly, he has also suggested the links between his ideas for a 'rhythomology of technology' to go with a rhythomology of music, dance and performance. Steve Beard, British cultural commentator, youth culture analyst and sometime novelist, and an uncannily accurate interpreter of Virilio himself (Beard 1998), has admitted that some, at least, of his own late 1990s fiction (or what he likes to call 'non-non-fiction'), like the 'rave' sequence in his novel *Digital Leatherette* (Beard 1999), was influenced by the mid 1990s theorisation of dance culture around Virilio's notion of 'the aesthetics of disappearance'. Writers such as Antonio Melechi and Hillegonda Rietveld, working at the Manchester Institute for Popular Culture, were responsible for the development of much of this work using Virilio's ideas while they were carrying out their own ethnographies into ecstasy (MDMA) use and dance culture around house music. Steve Beard 'fictionalised' some of the ideas coming out of the clash between the obscurantist notions produced by Paul Virilio in a completely different context and the fast-changing youth culture of the mid 1980s to mid 1990s. Steve Beard and his colleagues at British style magazine *i-D* 'applied' Virilio's ideas pervasively when writing about the cutting edges of what they labelled, and constructed as, 'style culture' from the 1980s onwards. Beard even took the notion of the 'logic bomb' as the title of an impressive collection of his own cultural journalism from the period. Semiotext(e)'s publications in the 'little black book' series, which could only be obtained in 1980s England in the Grass Roots bookshop in Manchester and the Compendium bookshop in London, were extremely influential in the development of left-field fiction writers in the 1980s and early 1990s such as Kathy Acker and Don Watson. This history of Virilio's influence is conveniently forgotten by those who wish to reinvent him as merely a high-cultural social theorist in the grand European tradition, or worse still a 'post-structuralist' or 'postmodernist' academic.

Against sociology

Whatever misgivings readers of his work have about the style of Virilio's writing, the focus of his work is, in reality, very wide.

Applications of his ideas to film, music, dance, military studies, law, international relations, philosophy, politics, visual art and architecture, as well as the human and social sciences in general, are plentiful in Virilio's writings. Even though the 'applications' are so unfinished and often simply peter out, the range of the fields itself is most impressive. Paul Virilio has made himself into a public intellectual of some standing over the years and he may eventually be remembered this way rather than as a general, or even subject-specific, theorist. Particularly in an age when world 'leaders' are of the quality and politics of George W. Bush, and 'commentators' in the fawning international media are ever more craven and un-critical, the fact that Virilio, as a liberal-humanist intellectual who speaks his mind, can find a place from which to pontificate is itself of great importance. His interventions in the 1990s on war in the Gulf and Balkans may point more to the long-lasting legacy of his work for understanding international relations, war and justice in the twenty-first century. The book *Strategy of Deception*, for exam-ple, was a contemporaneous intervention, originally published as articles in a German newspaper, on the NATO intervention in Kosovo at the end of the 1990s, which showed political courage and astute analysis on Virilio's part. It was also a perfectly readable little book aimed at a general audience rather than narrow academia. Reading *Strategy of Deception* a couple of years after the event, when it was published in English, it can be argued that Virilio's provocative stab at some of the hypocrisy of the USA and its allies stood up well to the test of time. Drawing on ideas partially developed in his various jottings in different books since the 'bunker archaeology' period, it was almost 'applied Virilio'!

Contrary to many commentators and critics' efforts in the past, the way to understand Virilio, we would submit in this book, is definitely not as a sociologist. Whatever liberal interpretation can be put on the boundaries of that discipline, the focus of the work of Virilio is not 'sociological' at all. He is not a social theorist in any conventional sense of the word. As he said in interview with Sylvère Lotringer, 'sociology, doesn't interest me'; 'I don't believe in sociology, I prefer politics and war'. Whereas Jean Baudrillard effectively gave up on sociology after 1968, Paul Virilio never even invested in it as a discipline in the first place. He has always believed that 'sociology was invented in order to forget politics'.

Moreover, there is a case for arguing that what Virilio has written about well is actually the 'disappearance' of the 'social'. That is, the 'social' in the sense that Virilio's fellow countryman Jacques Donzelot conceptualised the hybrid public/private sphere from the nineteenth century onwards in his book on the history and policing of the resultant 'social' domain. Donzelot's original French-language tract was translated into English in the late 1970s as *The Policing of Families*. In fact, Donzelot writes much more systematically and convincingly than Virilio does about this historical process and the implications for it of civil society, liberalism and governmentality. Politically, however, in some sympathetic treatments of his work Virilio is thought to offer some ways of thinking which might potentially roll back neo-liberalism and rebuild, in a different century, the 'social' domain which has 'disappeared'. The source of the disappearance of the social for Virilio is the fast-paced technologies which have brought about immediacy, instantaneousness and ubiquity with such a vengeance in such a short time, rather than the development of the market society per se. There are few places in Virilio where the idea of alternative social systems which minimise the harsher effects of markets are considered; there are even fewer where, in order to counter these market effects, a rebuilding of the modern secular state at national or regional level might be conceptualised and operationalised. In any case, Virilio has also always thought of the 'city' as the basis of politics. For him, 'politics is first and foremost the polis':

> Losing the city, we have lost everything. Recovering the city, we will have gained everything. If there is a solution possible today, it lies in reorganising the place of communal life. We must not let ourselves be betrayed or fooled by the tele-citta after the cine-citta. We must face the drama and tragedy of the city-world, this virtual city that delocalises work and our relationship to others. My solution is that of the urbanist in me. Working on the city, we will work on politics as well. In a way, this is a regression, since the word politics comes from polis, 'city'. We crashed into the wall, and we are now returning to the city. (Virilio 1999: 52)

This reorganisation of communal life is not simply a process of social engineering for Virilio. It is an intellectual project in itself.

Unfortunately, there are few resources for such a project in Virilio's body of work.

It is in Virilio's favour that he recognises that this is not merely an armchair 'philosophical' project. As he has said very clearly on a number of occasions, Virilio believes that 'philosophy is part of literature, and not the reverse, (and) writing is not possible without images'. Paul Virilio's writing is always an aesthetics as well as a cultural and social politics. Nevertheless, it is most clearly not part of a sociology or social theory (however critical) in any generally understood or accepted sense. It is somewhat ironic then that a book series like Sage's *Theory Culture and Society* (*TCS*), which published *Polar Inertia* in English translation, trumpeted Virilio as a contribution to 'social theory'. *TCS* also published John Armitage's edited collection of informative, if somewhat uneven and contradictory, essays on Virilio which labelled him a hyper-modernist and a contributor to a leftist 'techno politics'. Even though Armitage and the authors of some of the other outstanding contributions to the volume (like Mike Gane) appear self-consciously aware of the irony, the task of placing Paul Virilio in the pantheon of critical thought produced in Europe over the last fifty years is not greatly helped by trying to understand him as if he was a sociologist. Semiotext(e) remains the best site to pursue the enigma that is Paul Virilio. Reading carefully the *Pure War* interviews with Sylvère Lotringer from 1982 and 1997, or the equally insightful book-length interviews with Philippe Petit in *Politics of the Very Worst*, and then reading Virilio's texts themselves in the original, is a much better inroad into Virilio's life and work, especially for students wishing to begin an enquiry.

Globalisation in question?

For Paul Virilio the key to contemporary culture is that of a generalised 'arrival' (Crogan 1996). In other words, because every-thing is deemed to be happening in the instant present at the speed of light, there is no reason to actually go anywhere. The world is shrinking and a future of claustrophobia and inertia awaits us on earth, with possible warfare in space, if we are to follow Virilio at his most hyperbolic. The fact that we can travel to a world city like

'Tokyo in two hours on supersonic planes' will, for Virilio, bring more and more of the 'feeling of the world's narrowness' on a massive scale for the global population. 'The Earth', he has said, 'will still have a circumference of 40,000 kilometres, but it will not be travelled anymore'. For Virilio, 'it is hard to imagine the situation of confinement for the coming generations' and confinement in a world around us where history 'is hitting a cosmological limit – the cosmological constant of 300,000 kilometres per second'. We are now experiencing, in Virilio's analysis, the 'time of an Earth reduced to immediacy, instantaneity and ubiquity, a time reduced to the present, which is to say to what happens instantaneously'. With the worldwide revolution in communication and telematics in particular developing apace, 'acceleration has reached its physical limit, the speed of electromagnetic waves', according to Virilio. We are in the era of the accident of accidents, the total or general accident. A global accident would now affect if not the entire planet 'then at least the majority of people concerned by these teletechnologies' – as we have seen with the case study of 11 September 2001, this is exactly what has happened in some senses.

Much sociological and political debate through the 1990s, and into the early twenty-first century, has been couched in terms of the fashionable concept of 'globalisation'. Debates in politics and social science, for example, about the 'third way' – for and against – often turn on the extent to which social democratic or neo-liberal governments are able to influence what are pronounced to be 'global' processes beyond the control of national governments. The 'old' days of state socialism and *laissez-faire* capitalism are seen to be over for some believers in the 'third way' forward. Globalisation is frequently seen to be transforming the modern world in such a fundamental way – for instance, through the internet or world trade – that a completely new modernity is being born in the view of a growing band of theorists. The global economy is talked about as if it were a *fait accompli* and global culture accepted as if everyone had the internet, e-mail, a state of the art mobile phone or access to a McDonald's. Global democratic supranational governance is argued for as the only way to control the 'bad' effects of this globalisation.

As we have noted, globalisation has its adherents and its

opponents in the debate. Nation states are seen to have outlived their usefulness by those who adopt the standard globalisation perspective. For Paul Virilio, a supporter of transnationalisation, it is necessary to keep the centralisation of countries 'just long enough to surpass the Nation-state':

> The Nation-state is torn between two necessities. At the top, in the European Community, or even the world community, where the national state is surpassed by the possibility of a transnational state, and at the bottom by the will for a regional and decentralising emancipation. This double movement is suicidal for both democracy and politics. When the national state is pulled simultaneously at the top and bottom, there is no remaining transnational state and there is a movement towards the state of civil war, which is the case of the Eastern countries. We should have gone from a national state to a transnational state, skipping decentralisation, which could only occur in a transnational state. As soon as the state gave power to the regions, it lost its own power on a bigger scale and catastrophe was inevitable. I am in favour of transnationalisation or multinationalisation in Europe, but I am not in favour of simultaneous movement. (Virilio 1999: 76)

Dissenting voices in the globalisation debate, like the social theorist Paul Hirst and the economist Grahame Thompson, have claimed that nothing really fundamental has changed in the twentieth century, and that revolutions such as the telegraph in the nineteenth century or the systems of states and world trade emerging in the sixteenth and seventeenth centuries were actually more fundamental than the internet revolution. This argument has a lot to commend it. The book-length argument that Hirst himself makes for part of this position in *War and Power in the Twenty First Century* (Hirst 2001) would probably meet with Virilio's approval in some parts, but essentially there would be little common ground on many other issues. Hirst's book, centring on the history and future of warfare, technology and the state, does not make a single reference to any works by Virilio, despite his having written in this field for over thirty years. It is a salutary lesson that Virilio, however widespread his reputation has become, has remained a somewhat marginal figure in much scholarship about the topics he has addressed over the last thirty years. Virilio himself has always

been against the globalisation thesis, or at least been highly suspicious about it. He has blatantly said that 'the very word "globalisation" is a fake'. He has also insisted that 'there is no such thing as
globalisation, there is only virtualisation. What is being effectively
globalised by instantaneity is time.' In many ways Virilio's contribution to theorising what this book calls accelerated culture or
accelerated modernity has pitted the idea of acceleration against
globalisation as a more important and significant process in
modernity at the turn of the twentieth century. The political theorist
John Gray, who has argued the theme of 'de-globalisation' in the
wake of the 11 September 2001 attacks in New York and Washington, has captured Virilio's contribution to this debate on globalisation very well indeed without ever mentioning him by name:

> There is nothing unprecedented in the real changes the world
> economy is undergoing. The internet is only the latest in a series of
> technologies that began with the telegraph. There have been near-
> instantaneous link-ups between world markets ever since trans-
> atlantic underwater cables were laid in the last third of the nineteenth
> century. Looking further, we can see that today's new technologies
> are another phase in a worldwide industrial revolution that began
> 200 or 300 years ago ... The missionaries of globalisation failed to
> notice its darker side. They confused a genuinely inexorable
> historical process – the worldwide diffusion of new technologies
> that abolish or curtail time and distance – with market deregulation,
> a trend that is clearly on the wane. (*The Guardian*, 27 February 2001)

The new technologies 'that abolish or curtail time and distance' are
exactly the focus of Virilio's work and he certainly believes that the
'crisis' of the new technologies is no longer on just a city scale but
on 'a world scale'. However, unlike a theorist like John Gray,
Virilio – as we have already emphasised – has little to say about the
contribution of markets and the relationship of the 'e-conomy' (or
new economy, where the communications revolution has had such
an impact on time and distance) to the traditional economy in
various countries throughout the globe. Moreover, Virilio's arguments about time and distance melting away, however initially
seductive, are at such a level of rhetoric and generality that all the
specific and local changes in economics and technology, especially
at the level of regional and national states, are completely neglected.

Contemporary thinker

Not content with the numerous books he has already published Paul Virilio continued to produce new work in the new century. In late 2000, when Virilio was aged sixty-eight, *La Procédure Silence* became his latest French-language text to hit the Paris bookshops. Eventually, in 2003, Continuum Books published an English translation (Virilio 2003a) with the cryptic but appropriate title *Art and Fear*. Appropriately, given his stance against sociology, *La Procédure Silence* would probably not be classed as sociological in any language. It was, as so often in the past with all his works, hard to pigeonhole. As the international academic world re-erected disciplinary boundaries in its retreat from the idea of liberal education for its own sake, a theorist like Paul Virilio has continued to smash down the boundaries with aplomb. Published as usual by Galilée in Paris in the 'Collection L'Espace Critique' series, *La Procédure Silence* (echoing the passive acceptance of the NATO war in the 1990s) was ostensibly the regular, incisive 'pithy' Virilio book, this time about 'the contemporary crisis in art'. But it remained, in effect, as much a treatise about the 'merciless' or *'impitoyable'* twentieth century that had disappeared and the new and dangerous century on the horizon; in other words, it was about 'art and fear', or more specifically about the twin developments of art and science over the twentieth century. Divided into two parts, it was again a short book, this time of only seventy-five pages in the original French. The first section was entitled 'Un Art Impitoyable' and the second 'La Procédure Silence'. The book quoted Albert Camus' phrase 'le XX siècle, ce siècle impitoyable' and cited all kinds of 'fin de siècle' references from Greil Marcus' tour de force on the Situationists, punk rock and the Sex Pistols, *Lipstick Traces*, to the writing of German theorist Hans Magnus Enzensberger. Discussion ranged over cultural figures as diverse as Mark Rothko, Guy Debord, Stelarc, Picasso and Marshall McLuhan. The book demonstrated that the contemporary crisis in art ('l'art contemporain est en crise' screamed the 'cool', modernist, cream cover in France), for Paul Virilio, has clearly not been comprehensible without a clear understanding of the effect of the terror, or fear, of the twentieth century (or, as we have regularly noted, the century of 'hyper-violence' as memorably christened by Virilio). 'Terror', and especially what Virilio calls 'state terrorism', from Hitler to Pol Pot, has impacted on all the artistic works, on all representation, of that merciless period of human history, according to Virilio. As the back-cover 'blurb' of the French edition of the book puts it, 'sans le terreur, les œuvres du XX siècle sont impensables, invisibles même. Sans la montée des périls, le drame des apparences contemporaines est incompréhensible, répréhensible selon certains'. Art, moreover, for Virilio in this book saw itself being replaced by 'science' or 'technoscience', where experimental science becomes one with technology as the chronicler of the anxiety of our times at the beginning of the twenty-first century. 'La Technoscience inaugure un expressionnisme', as Galilée's summary put it. Art's crisis in Virilio's view reflects the 'wages of fear' – 'le salaire de la peur' – created by the twentieth century. Hence, the book's overall title *La Procédure Silence* – a phrase already familiar to readers of Virilio from *Strategy of Deception* – which means, in rough English translation, giving the 'green light by implicit consensus'. In Virilio's short, punchy text, art and science rival each other for the eventual destruction of the human form, art in its myriad types of representation and science with its genetic engineering.

The continuing 'elusiveness' of Virilio partly relates to the difficulty of labelling him. This usually leads to simplification or reification, and both have happened in Virilio's reception as a theorist in the international academy. In turn, this desire to simplify or reify breeds cult status. Like many French theorists before him, and no doubt many still to come afterwards, Paul Virilio himself has been subject to 'aestheticisation' or 'fetishisation'. Like Gilles Deleuze and Félix Guattari in the 1990s, Michel Foucault in the 1980s, Louis Althusser in the 1970s, or Guy Debord in the 1960s, Paul Virilio has become a name to drop. He seems himself to be remarkably unaffected by all the academic and media attention in his own country, and now more regularly on the world stage. Whether Virilio's work will last in the twenty-first century, compared to that of the likes of Michel Foucault, and whether it will give rise to major sustained interrogations within the academy is debatable. But there is no doubt that there will be significant debate. The media and academic attention which has now come his way is partly due to the burial of so much of his work over the last thirty years when it might have been more appropriately received.

Cultural theorists cite Virilio now as they once did the better-known French figures of high modernist academic theory. The visual art world notes him too. He has himself been involved in exhibitions and written copy for catalogues over the years. As we have seen in this book, 'La Vitesse' and 'Ce Qui Arrive' were successful exhibitions for the Fondation Cartier in France. The catalogue for the exhibition 'Speed – Visions of an Accelerated Age', held at the Whitechapel Art Gallery and the Photographers' Gallery in London in 1998, contained an artily framed reprint of Virilio's essay 'The Last Vehicle', a paper first presented to a symposium which included Jean Baudrillard as a fellow presenter in New York in 1986 and the proceedings of which Semiotext(e) published in its 'little black book' series under the title *Looking Back on the End of the World*. Wherever there is what Douglas Coupland once prophetically and astutely labelled 'accelerated culture' in his prophetic subtitle for the best-selling fiction work *Generation X: Tales for an Accelerated Culture*, there you will now frequently find the name of Paul Virilio. He is justly regarded as a contemporary cultural thinker. But unlike the earlier French theoretical superstars, Virilio is really the antithesis of the trendy, the fashionable and the celebrated. As this book has made clear, he has been committed, over a very long period, to an analysis (however flawed) of what this book has variously conceptualised as accelerated, dangerous and critical modernity with a much greater consistency than his more esteemed French counterparts. He has been in it for 'the long haul' for more than forty years, and arguably even more if the early pioneering studies of the bunkers are taken into account. He is not so much a prophet of apocalypse, more, as he has said, a 'true lover of the new technologies', a perverse theorist of the 'cybernetic technologies'. These techno-logies are, he has said, 'as well as the media in the broadest sense' like the 'German Occupation'. Still fighting the Second World War as always, Virilio has labelled his own work as 'that of a "resister"' because there are too many "collaborators" who are once again pulling the trick of redemptory progress, emancipation, man liber-ated from all repression etc'. The 'early' early Virilio, the child influenced by the trauma of the Second World War, acutely feeling the 'claustrophobic' effects of the Allied bombing against the German-held France which was his homeland, is always present in this long haul of the older, grown-up Paul Virilio.

Bunker man

Virilio has undoubtedly been an elusive theorist of speed, dipping in and out of debates about all kinds of topics, but the one consistent 'disciplinary' area in terms of his academic appointment and teaching over the last thirty years has been architecture. As we have seen in this book, despite his professorship in architecture for thirty years, Virilio was not an architect by professional training, but more in socialisation through his friendship and working relationship in the 1960s with his erstwhile partner Claude Parent. As architecture gained a trendiness as the 'new rock'n'roll' in the late 1990s when superstar architects like Rem Koolhaas and Daniel Libeskind, from a younger generation than Paul Virilio, began to achieve previously unheard-of global fame, Virilio himself in this period blossomed internationally as a public intellectual. In turn, global academic cultural theory in the late 1990s, and its international conference circuit, increasingly turned to architecture and to celebrity architects like Koolhaas and Libeskind for a supposedly new perspective, as if they were social theorists. Keynote addresses, normally given by academics, were often presented by the celebrity architects themselves who had been suddenly thrust into the limelight for their 'theories'. Virilio, who has kept a relatively low profile in comparison, must have felt that he had seen it all before, for he has been quoted and appropriated as an architecture academic-cum-cultural theorist for thirty years. There are, too, what feel like rather 'spooky' echoes of Paul Virilio today in architectural debates. Daniel Libeskind's buildings like the Imperial War Museum North in Salford, Greater Manchester, for instance, sometimes have inclined floors. Libeskind, the architect who successfully won the design competition to rebuild a modernist 'memorial' structure on the space previously occupied by the twin towers of the World Trade Center, was himself a contributor to the tenth Virilio and Parent *Architecture*

Principe papers in 1996. These papers included, in English, a number of contemporary architectural contributions from the likes of Bernard Tschumi, who, as we have seen already in this book, penned the foreword to the English edition of *A Landscape of Events*, and Jean Nouvel about whom Virilio himself published a pamphlet. Still to gain real international recognition in the mid 1990s, something which was to come soon enough, Daniel Libeskind submitted to the 1996 collection an essay on the need to resist the erasure of history, a paper called 'Traces of the Unborn'. It could have been the younger Virilio writing in an earlier period in the 1960s.

Paul Virilio's general theoretical work, rather than his writings on architecture itself, and especially his work on the aesthetics of disappearance, has had major implications for architecture as a discipline as cultural theorists re-engage in the twenty-first century with the Virilio and Parent notion of critical modernity from the twentieth century. As he told Andreas Ruby in 1993 in interview:

> First of all, the disappearance not only affects architecture but any kind of materiality: the earth (deterritorialisation), the body (disembodiment) and architecture (deconstruction – in the literal sense of the word, not the architectural style). Any kind of matter is about to vanish in favour of information. You can see it also as a change of aesthetics. To me, to disappear does not mean to become eliminated. Just like the Atlantic, which continues to be there even though you can no longer feel it as you fly over it. Or like the body that continues to exist without actually being needed – since we just switch the channel. The same happens with architecture: it will continue to exist, but in the state of disappearance. (Beckmann 1998c: 186–7)

'Architecture' as a word has become, in Virilio's vocabulary, unnecessary. As he has said, 'high technology' is sufficient to describe 'high tech architecture' with 'many architects' using the vocabulary 'of 'airplanes or space shuttles'. For Virilio, at least in his thought process of the early 1990s, 'architecture is just about to lose everything that characterised it in the past'. He felt that 'step by step it loses all its elements' even anticipating the media buildings in some Asian and other continents' cities with façades entirely made of screen. For Virilio 'in a certain sense, the screen becomes the last wall'. In a sense, Virilio's contribution to the understanding of accelerated, dangerous and critical modernity has been all of a piece in the ultimate analysis. His argument has been, to oversimplify somewhat whilst using his own words, that 'stability has become less important than speed today' or 'that what happens is much more important than that which lasts – and also than that which is solid'. As we have said before in this book, he has written the footnote to Marx's idea of modernity. Furthermore, the virtual dimension is crucial to the future of architecture and to Virilio's theoretical suggestiveness. As he argued to Andreas Ruby:

> The space of the future would be both of real and virtual nature. Achitecture will 'take place' in the literal sense of the word, in both domains: in real space (the materiality of architecture) and virtual space (the transmission of electromagnetic signs). The real space of the house will have to take into account the real time of the transmission. (Beckmann, 1998c: 182–3)

This duplication of reality which Virilio controversially puts forward as a general thesis reminds us that time is 'one of the hidden issues in the history of architecture'. It also emphasises that today society is 'split up, not by light but by speed: one part still lives in an electrical world, the other in an electronic world'. In this argument Virilio believes that 'the first lives within the relative speed (of mechanical transportation, for example) while the second participates in the absolute speed (of the transmission of information in real time, for example)'.

As a footnote to our case study of the accident of accidents in Chapter 3, it is worth remembering how much of Virilio's early work was present in the later. After the hijacked airliners' suicide attack on what were previously the most famous skyscrapers of New York on 11 September 2001, the British architect Norman Foster noted that 'skyscrapers are not going to go away. What do we do if we don't build high? Give up and live in bunkers? And then fret about nerve gas?' He might have been thinking, unconsciously of course, of Paul Virilio, the 'bunker man', when he made these statements. There are certainly 'traces' of Virilio in many different areas and disciplines, not just architecture, and this quotation from Foster indicates, uncannily, Paul Virilio's synchronicity with the times. We might not remember much about Paul Virilio — after all, there are so many theorists and theories to absorb and they are so diverse, as Jean Baudrillard reminds us — but we certainly forget him at our peril. Yet forget him we must.

Forget Virilio

This book concludes with the view that after all is said and done, we do probably have to forget Virilio for all sorts of reasons. These include the trajectory of those who were involved in 'May '68' and their conceptions of the state and governance, and the notions of human nature, sexuality and subjectivity which have been re-worked so extensively since the 1950s. Virilio, unlike many of his European intellectual contemporaries, did not lurch to the right after 1968, during the 1970s and 1980s, and he has maintained a reasonably consistent liberal-humanist position for most of the three decades he has been writing and speaking after the poten-tially monumental upheavals of the May 1968 events.

An instructive comparison in this regard is with someone like the Italian Marxist philosopher Lucio Colletti, another theorist of Virilio's generation with an Italian father. Colletti, a few years older than Virilio, was born in 1924. He joined the PCI (Italian Com-munist Party) in the 1950s but dissented from the Communist Party-led Soviet Union invasion of Hungary in 1956. Later, in the 1960s, Colletti took over the mantle, left behind by his mentor Galvano Della Volpe, one of the best-known living Italian Marxist philosophers of the time. He held a chair in philosophy at the university of Rome during the 1960s. But Colletti was against the movement of 'May '68' and became marginalised despite his com-mitment to theoretically justifying a scientific basis for Marxism in books like *From Rousseau to Lenin* and *Marxism and Hegel*. By 1974 Colletti had turned his back on Marxism and he effectively moved straight on to the politics of market socialism of the PSI (Italian Socialist Party), feeling no sympathy for the 'Eurocommunism' of Enrico Berlinguer and the changing face of the PCI. However, after the fall of Eastern European communism in the 1980s, Colletti lurched into the arms of the party led by capitalist media magnate Silvio Berlusconi. For the last few years of his life Colletti sat in the

Italian parliament as a deputy in Berlusconi's 'Forza Italia' right-wing party. Not so much from Rousseau to Lenin, as from Marx to Berlusconi! Paul Virilio, in contradistinction to Lucio Colletti, has always thought very differently about the politics of Silvio Berlusconi and his ilk. He has said that 'Berlusconi, after Ross Perot, succeeded in breaking the barrier of politics and, for the first time in recent history, the opposition was no longer between the left and the right, but between the media and politics'. In stark contrast to the past of a theorist like Colletti, Paul Virilio, who was outside academia until 1968, became galvanised by the events of 'May '68' and owed his entry into the academy to the students' and workers' movement. But Virilio played no formal part in a labour movement after this period. Virilio was no Communist Party intellectual like Louis Althusser, although his own father was an Italian Communist. Interestingly, however, Althusser took up the issue of the 'military aspect' of the French Communist Party (namely their strategy of secrecy and policing of the party), and Virilio cited it as 'taking up rather faithfully the theses of my book *Speed and Politics*'. As we have emphasised in this book, Virilio was no Trotskyist or anarchist either. He has said too that he has been 'no ecologist in the Green party sense'. As an academic he has spent his intellectual life as a Professor of Architecture for thirty years from 1969 and as an independent writer and thinker for even longer. This meant that he was unconnected to any of the currents in French, and indeed wider European, politics in the subsequent thirty years. Virilio could be seen in Paris in the company of the likes of Baudrillard and Guattari (and to be mentioned in the same context as Deleuze) as well as some of those who were seen in France as more reactionary like Joxe and Glucksmann, without necessarily incurring the wrath of one wing or the other in French political and public life. One of his mentors as a young man forty years ago at the university of the Sorbonne was the sociologist Raymond Aron, an influential thinker for 'moderates' and conservatives in France at a time when the left was dominated by the likes of Jean-Paul Sartre. The existentialist Marxism of Sartre was something Virilio never embraced; Virilio's 'phenomenological' upbringing was of a somewhat different vintage, as we have seen. Furthermore, Jacques Ellul, theologian and philosopher of technology, was a background influence until his death in 1994 and Virilio has explicitly stated that he was in some ways carrying on Ellul's work. However, all of this meant that Virilio's furrow was a lone one, and that comprehensive and contextual analysis of current conditions was never really developed at all by Virilio. 'Events', as he has admitted, spawned his writing, thinking and interventions, not a theoretical or political context or biography.

The state in Virilio's thinking, as is the case for many of the generation of 'May '68', also causes problems for his theoretical and political work. He has been anti-statist in much of his writing, and his Catholicism complicates his attitude to the modern formation of the secular state in European countries like France over several centuries. As Patrick Crogan has argued, 'Virilio does not have an explicitly formulated theory of the state', although he does talk of a 'Pure State' to go along with 'Pure War'. Speed and war, and their acceleration in the post-Second World War period, are the processes on which Virilio has concentrated, not a rigorous conceptualising of the state, or of governance, in that period. Whilst Louis Althusser was developing a very different kind of scientific basis for Marxist theory in the 1960s and 1970s in France to that of Lucio Colletti in Italy, and conceptualising the 'repressive' and 'ideological' state apparatuses, Virilio was studiously avoiding theoretical questions surrounding the formation of the state. Nevertheless, his writing is peppered with anecdotal evidence of what the state in any geographical context actually does at any one time in history. This is mainly connected to his concentration on uncovering the state of 'Pure War', or in other words the 'perpetuation of war' in the period since the Second World War. So Virilio has garnered many stories about, say, the Pentagon or the Kremlin, and the revolution in war technology over the years, but he has barely theorised these structures anew on any scale. Virilio, however, has occasionally illuminated one or two aspects of the modern state in his writing. He has described and analysed the 'turning a state of war into a war against one's own population' by the term 'endocolonisation'; that is, the colonisation imperative turned in on itself. As Virilio has pointed out, 'one now only colonises one's own population'. With this, for Virilio, came the 'minimum state': the idea that 'you concentrate power on war, on economic and military-industrial development etc. and you let the rest drop dead'. Virilio also conceived the 'suicide state' where 'terror' spreads over an entire country and the state 'disappears', and he cited the example of Cambodia under Pol Pot in the 1970s as an instance of this process. In general, however, Virilio has made his contribution to the theory of state formations more by his concentration on what that whole body of theoretical work left out – war and speed.

As we have seen earlier in this book, the 'picnolept', the subject of picnolepsy (the state of tiny death), or the figure able to live outside clock time or to disappear from militarised time for a fleeting moment, represents Virilio's contribution to theories of subjectivity. He has, however, not formulated such a notion rigorously or pursued it at great length in his work, although it is important in passing to his project of forging an 'aesthetics of disappearance'. Picnolepsy has little connection to the other contemporary ways of seeing the self or subjectivity in the human or social sciences. Picnolepsy, for example, in Virilio's oeuvre is not comparable to Michel Foucault's multi-volume project on the 'history of sexuality' with its notions of technologies of the self and massive historical shifts. In keeping with Virilio's projected aim in general in his work it is 'suggestive' and 'implicit'. Again, in comparison with Michel Foucault, the notion of the body, and indeed human nature, in Virilio's thinking is pre-technological, pre-existing the formations of sexuality and the social.

Scream if you want to go faster

In final conclusion to this book it is clear that the name of Paul Virilio will always be associated with the word 'speed'. The colloquial name for the street drug amphetamine will never register a connection with Virilio, but just about every other way of entering the term into the search engines of the internet will throw up Paul Virilio's name. But, as some critics have suggested, theory itself is speeding up. The speed of theory, the speed of writing, the speed of seeing are all important facets of modernity, accelerated or dangerous or critical. As Virilio has pointed out, speed is vital to our ways of seeing, what John Armitage has called the 'vision thing' (Armitage 1996). Virilio has proclaimed that 'speed enables you to see. It does not simply allow you to arrive at your destination more quickly, rather it enables you to see and foresee.' Whether the way Virilio has written and thought (about) speed has moved beyond that of other theorists remains a debate that is far from closed after the investigations undertaken in this book. He has said that he does not believe in 'explanations' but 'suggestions', so the form of the writing is crucial for conveying the implicitness of speed in culture. Virilio's argument has been explicitly that he has not valued 'two-and-two-is-four-type of writing' and that is why 'finally' Virilio can say he respected Michel Foucault more than he liked him! This 'writing (of) speed' involves for Virilio a 'whole politics of writing'. Virilio has openly admitted:

> I work in staircases – some people have realised this. I begin a sentence. I work out an idea and when I consider it suggestive enough, I jump a step to another idea without bothering with the development. Developments are the episodes. I try to reach the tendency. Tendency is the change of level … I handle breaks and absences. The fact of stopping and saying 'let's go somewhere else' is very important for me. (Virilio 1997a: 44–5)

The eschewing of two-and-two-is-four-type of writing by Virilio is perhaps why some critics and readers of his work find it to be illogically put together. Yet for others it is part of the charm and the seduction of his writing and speaking.

Perhaps Virilio is, in the final analysis, a curious choice of theorist, as I have coined it in this book, for an accelerated culture. After all, he has described one of his books, *The Aesthetics of Disappearance*, as having as its main idea 'the social and political role of stopping'. Sedentariness and going nowhere in the face of blinding light is often his focus. Also, he is in so many ways backward-looking, however humanistically, a very traditional figure frozen in the history of the Second World War and a quite formal Christianity suspicious of what technological revolutions can do to human existence. As he announced to Sylvère Lotringer in 1997:

> The great combat is between transcendent God and God-machine. We should be able to talk about this, but we can't. It's not politically correct. I can talk about it with Christians, but not with

anyone else. And I'm fed up with that. We should be able to talk about sex, angels, God, everything. The world has arrived at an extremity where things need to be sorted out. Have they survived the fire or what? When do we cut the umbilical cord? We're backed into a corner, too, you see. All of us. Not simply a death impasse, but stuck in the corner as a result of globalisation and everything we've been describing. It's the end of an era. It's the end of a temporal regime, and hence a regime of thought. Philosophy was inscribed in historical time, whereas today, in the new historical time, this real time has no thought. It can have non-thought, in other words, a negation. Nihilism could be its Assumption in times to come, far beyond what fascism and nazism were and that's the great temptation. In that case you can't be a collaborator. That's why I'm saying that you can collaborate or resist faced with this situation. The thing about collaborators is that you don't know you are one, whereas as a member of the resistance, you do. To be in the resistance, you choose to be in it. If I take the Second World War as an example, the worst cases of collaboration weren't among the real collaborators, the official Militia, but among the populace at large, who were collaborators without knowing it, by a sort of laxity, an apathy. (Virilio 1997a: 182–3)

Paul Virilio, like anyone else, is entitled to his personal religious or spiritual faith. Where it becomes a problem is when it pervades the framework of a thinker's ideas. In Arthur Kroker's (Kroker 1992) assessment of Virilio alongside other theorists, the 'dissenting' Catholicism is awarded a purpose. We have noted in the course of this book a more limiting function of formal Christianity on the impact and scope of Virilio's thinking, conversation and writing. As he has said himself, however, 'my work is that of a limited man who must deal with a limitless situation'. Paul Virilio is, in his own words, a 'man who started to take an interest in speed when the limit of speed was being reached, 300,000 kilometres per second'. Certainly, in the areas we have looked at in this book under the rubric of the development of concepts such as accelerated, dangerous and critical modernity, Virilio has sometimes made a distinctive contribution as an important contemporary thinker. It would be difficult to think of theorising speed, technology and modernity without some consideration of the work of Virilio. Whether he has been able to lead us into a more incisive way of capturing the 'new' or critical modernity on our horizons is definitely a much more open and perplexing question to answer. We shall have to sit, inertly, in what Virilio has idiosyncratically labelled this age of 'crepuscular dawn', watching our screens, and wait and see. I, for one, am not holding my breath.

Bibliography

Selected works, available in English, by Paul Virilio

Note: * indicates that the work is only available in electronic form.

Virilio, P. 2003a: *Art and Fear*. London: Continuum.
Virilio, P. 2003b: *Unknown Quantity*. London: Thames and Hudson.
Virilio, P. 2002a: *Ground Zero*. London: Verso.
Virilio, P. 2002b: *Crepuscular Dawn*. New York: Semiotext(e).
Virilio, P. 2002c: *Desert Screen: War at the Speed of Light*. London: Continuum.
Virilio, P. 2000a: *Strategy of Deception*. London: Verso.
Virilio, P. 2000b: *A Landscape of Events*. Cambridge: MIT Press.
Virilio, P. 2000c: *The Information Bomb*. London: Verso.
Virilio, P. 2000d: *Polar Inertia*. London: Sage.
Virilio, P. 1999: *Politics of the Very Worst*. New York: Semiotext(e).
Der Derian, J. (ed.) 1998: *The Virilio Reader*. Oxford: Blackwell.
Virilio, P. 1997a: *Pure War*, 2nd edn. New York: Semiotext(e).
Virilio, P. 1997b: *Open Sky*. London: Verso.
Virilio, P. and Parent, C. 1997: *Architecture Principe 1966 and 1996*. Paris: Les Editions de L'Imprimeur.
Virilio, P. and Parent, C. 1996: *The Function of the Oblique: The Architecture of Claude Parent and Paul Virilio 1963–1969*. London: Architectural Association.
Virilio, P. 1995a: *The Art of the Motor*. Minneapolis: University of Minnesota Press.
Virilio, P. 1995b: Speed and Information: Cyberspace Alarm! *Ctheory*.*
Virilio, P. 1994a: *The Vision Machine*. London: British Film Institute.
Virilio, P. 1994b: *Bunker Archaeology*. New York: Princeton Architectural Press.
Virilio, P. 1993a: 'The Third Interval: A Critical Transition', in V. A. Conley (ed.), *Rethinking Technologies*. Minneapolis: University of Minnesota Press.
Virilio, P. 1991a: *The Aesthetics of Disappearance*. New York: Semiotext(e).

Virilio, P. 1991b: *The Lost Dimension*. New York: Semiotext(e).

Virilio, P. 1990a: *Popular Defense and Ecological Struggles*. New York: Semiotext(e).

Virilio, P. 1990b: 'Cataract Surgery: Cinema in the Year 2000', in A. Kuhn (ed.), *Alien Zone: Cultural Theory and Contemporary Science Fiction Cinema*. London: Verso.

Virilio, P. 1989a: 'The Last Vehicle', in D. Kamper and C. Wulf (eds), *Looking Back on the End of the World*. New York: Semiotext(e).

Virilio, P. 1989b: *War and Cinema: The Logistics of Perception*. London: Verso.

Virilio, P. 1987: 'Negative Horizons', in *Semiotext(e): USA*. New York: Semiotext(e).

Virilio, P. 1986: *Speed and Politics: An Essay on Dromology*. New York: Semiotext(e).

Virilio, P. 1981: 'Moving Girl', in *Semiotext(e): Polysexuality*. New York: Semiotext(e).

Selected works, untranslated or partially translated, available only in full in French, by Paul Virilio

Virilio, P. 1997c: *Voyage d'Hiver*. Marseille: Parentheses.

Virilio, P. 1993b: *L'Insécurité du Territoire*, 2nd edn. Paris: Galilée.

Virilio, P. 1978: *La Dromoscopie ou la Lumière de la Vitesse*. Paris: Editions de Minuit.

Selected interviews, available in English, with Paul Virilio

2002: Interviews with Sylvère Lotringer, in *Crepuscular Dawn*. New York: Semiotext(e).

2001a: Selected interviews, in J. Armitage (ed.), *Virilio Live*. London: Sage.

2001b: A Crash of Strategic Thought? *hydrarchist*.*

2000a: The Kosovo War took place in Orbital Space: Interview with John Armitage. *Ctheory*.*

2000b: From Modernism to Hypermodernism and Beyond: Interview with John Armitage, in J. Armitage (ed.), *Paul Virilio: From Modernism to Hypermodernism and Beyond*. London: Sage.

1999a: Interviews with Philippe Petit, in *Politics of the Very Worst*. New York: Semiotext(e).

1999b: The Information Bomb: A Conversation with Friedrich Kittler. *Angelaki* 4, 2.

1998a: Surfing the Accident: Interview with Andreas Ruby, in A. Broekman et al. (eds), *The Art of the Accident*. Rotterdam: NAI Publishers.

1998b: Is the Author Dead? Interview with James Der Derian, in J. Der Derian (ed.), *The Virilio Reader*. Oxford: Blackwell.

1998c: Architecture in the Age of its Virtual Disappearance: Interview with Andreas Ruby, in J. Beckmann (ed.), *The Virtual Dimension*. New York: Princeton Architectural Press.

1996a: A Century of Hyperviolence: Interview with Nicholas Zurbrugg. *Economy And Society* 25, 1.

1996b: Cyberesistance Fighter: Interview with David Dufresne. *Après Coup*.*

1995: The Silence of the Lambs: Interview with Carlos Oliveira. *Ctheory*.*

1994: Cyberwar, God and Television: Interview with Louise Wilson. *Ctheory* (printed in 1997: A. Kroker and M. Kroker (eds), *Digital Delirium*. New York: St Martin's Press).

1983: Interviews with Sylvère Lotringer, in *Pure War*. New York: Semiotext(e) (2nd edition in 1997 incorporates a new interview with Sylvère Lotringer as an Afterword).

Selected commentaries, available in English, on Paul Virilio

Armitage, J. 2000a: 'Editorial Introduction'. *Angelaki*, 4, 2.

Armitage, J. 2000b: *Paul Virilio: From Modernism to Hypermodernism and Beyond*. London: Sage.

Armitage, J. 2000c: 'Paul Virilio: La Bombe Informatique'. *New Left Review*, 2.

Armitage, J. 1997: 'Accelerated Aesthetics'. *Angelaki*, 2, 3.

Armitage, J. 1996: 'The Vision Thing'. *Radical Philosophy*, 77.

Baudrillard, J. 2000: Interview, in M. Sanders and J. Hack (eds), *Star Culture*. London: Phaidon.

Beard, S. 1999: *Digital Leatherette*. Hove: Codex.

Beard, S. 1998: *Logic Bomb*. London: Serpent's Tail.

Bosworth, R. 1993: *Explaining Auschwitz and Hiroshima*. London: Routledge.

Brigham, L. 1996: 'Transpolitical Technocracy and the Hope of Language: Virilio and Habermas', in *Speed*, 1. 4 (Special Issue on Virilio).*

Chomsky, N. 2001: *September 11*. Crows Nest: Allen and Unwin.

Crawford, T. H. 2000: 'Conducting Technologies: Virilio's and Latour's Philosophies of the Present State'. *Angelaki*, 4, 2.

Crogan, P. 2000: 'Theory of State: Deleuze, Guattari and Virilio on the State, Technology and Speed'. *Angelaki*, 4, 2.

Crogan, P. 1996: *The Aporia of Speed*. Paper to Virtual Cultures Conference, Sydney.*

Cubitt, S. 2001: *Simulation and Social Theory*. London: Sage.

Cubitt, S. 1999: 'Unnatural Reality.' *Film-Philosophy: Electronic Salon*.*

Der Derian, J. 1998: 'Introduction', in J. Der Derian (ed.), *The Virilio Reader*. Oxford: Blackwell.

Douglas, I. 1996: 'The Calm before the Storm: Virilio's Debt to Foucault and Some Notes on Contemporary Global Capital'. *Speed*, 1. 4 (Special Issue on Virilio).*

Featherstone, M. and Lash, S. (eds) 1999: *Spaces of Culture*. London: Sage.

Gane, M. 1993: *Baudrillard Live*. London: Routledge.

Genosko, G. (ed.) 2001: *The Uncollected Baudrillard*. London: Sage.

Hirst, P. 2001: *War and Power in the Twenty First Century*. Cambridge: Polity.

Kellner, D. 1998: 'Virilio on Vision Machines.' *Film-Philosophy: Electronic Salon*.*

Kroker, A. 1992: *The Possessed Individual*. Basingstoke: Macmillan.

Luke, T. 1998: 'Moving at the Speed of Life? A Critical Kinematics of Telematic Times and Corporate Values', in S. Lash et al. (eds), *Time and Value*. Oxford: Blackwell.

Lury, C. 1998: *Prosthetic Culture*. London: Routledge.

Patrick, K. 2003: 'The Century of Fear'. *Contemporary*, no. 47/48.

Peters, P. 2000: 'Parallel Velocities'. *Theory, Culture And Society*, 17, 6.

Silverman, M. 1999: *Facing Postmodernity*. London: Routledge.

Sokal, A. and Bricmont, J. 1999: *Intellectual Impostures*. London: Profile Books.

Telotte, J. 1999: 'Verhoeven, Virilio and Cinematic Derealization'. *Film Quarterly*, Winter.

Wark, M. 1988: 'On Technological Time: Cruising Virilio's Over-Exposed City'. *Arena*, 83.

Wilbur, S. 1994: 'Dromologies: Paul Virilio: Speed, Cinema and the End of the Political State'.*

Index